GUN DOG CHRONICLES

*Reflections on Upland Bird Dogs
and Waterfowl Retrievers*

GUN DOG CHRONICLES

*Reflections on Upland Bird Dogs
and Waterfowl Retrievers*

by

Joe Arnette

Prologue by
Joel Vance

Original artwork by
Ross B. Young

Silver Quill Press
Camden / Maine

Copyright © 2001 Joe Arnette
Jacket Illustrations and Line Drawings © 2001 Ross B. Young

Printed at Versa Press, East Peoria, IL

5   4   3   2   1

ISBN 0-89272-530-3

Library of Congress Control Number 2001089042

Silver Quill Press is an imprint of
Down East Books
P.O. Box 679
Camden, Maine 04843
Book Orders: 1-800-685-7962
www.downeastbooks.com

Contents

Part III — The Last Years

Epilogue

Gun Dog Chronicles

Prologue

by
Joel Vance

Not long ago, Joe Arnette and I were rooming together at a Kansas hunting lodge whose owners had the eminent good sense to let the hunters sleep with their dogs.

Joe's beloved springers were at home in Maine because of the trip distance, but I had Flick, a fun-loving French Brittany. Bedtime came, and I waited for Flick to come be my warm sleep toy.

Instead he sneered at me, leaped on Joe's bed, smiled at him with boundless love, sighed contentedly, and went to sleep.

Obviously here was a man who had a deep affinity with dogs. As you're about to find out, he also has a deep affinity with good writing, a rarity in the world of outdoor reportage. He flat knows how to string words together and to make them entertaining and informative.

Wildlife biologists tend to know their territory; writers tend to know theirs. It's rare to find a wildlife biologist who also can write. John Madson did it superlatively, as did Rachel Carson . . . and Joe Arnette is another of that rare breed.

Come along with Joe and his dogs, and find out what it's all about in the field. You won't regret the trip, and you won't have to endure (except vicariously) the sweat and briars, the blowdowns, and the mudholes of the real thing.

It's the best of all possible worlds—being there through the magic of a fine writer's words, but doing it within the comfort of your favorite reading chair.

Joe and I share column space in *Gun Dog* magazine, where I fulminate about the idiot doings of politicians in the world of conservation. Joe gets to write the back page, that sacred spot where columnists leave you with a good feeling. Editors pick their best writers for the back-page column, and selecting Joe to do "Parting Shots" was an inspired choice.

If I hadn't already been given my own conservation column in the middle of the magazine, I'd have been jealous; as it is, I make 'em mad, and Joe soothes them at the end. It's a talent at which he is a master.

Flick fell off the bed in the middle of the night and landed on Joe's gun case, which reverberated in the small room like a cannon. I was startled awake, my heart pounding. I was sure we'd been attacked by foreign powers, but Joe merely said in the dark, "Come on Flick. It's okay—let's go back to sleep."

There was the rustling sound of a dog snuggling up, and then there was—as there always is when Joe is around—contentment and satisfaction.

Let's go see what those dogs are up to. . . .

Preface

In good part, this book is a historical sampler of my experiences with gun dogs: my personal hunting companions, those of friends and acquaintances, and—in some cases—those belonging to strangers. But *Gun Dog Chronicles* is not about me. It concerns my life only by way of the hunting dogs that have been part of it. Whether I speak to you directly or through the eyes and heart of another, my role in this book is that of narrator.

The chronology of these tales stretches over most of a lifetime, from my wide-eyed, prepubescent fascination with the gun dogs owned by my family to my deep appreciation of today's dogs. The book is organized into three sections, structured around the main stages in a dog's life—youth, maturity, and old age.

Much of this chronicling is true. That said, names, locations, and times have been altered in most of the stories out of consideration for the participants. The details of some experiences have become casualties of the passing years and required imaginative reconstruction. Still other adventures might not have happened exactly as I present them here, but they could have or damn well should have. A few of these tales are pure invention, albeit written around a core of truth or an actual event.

A number of these pieces originally appeared as columns and feature articles in national magazines. However, all such essays have been revised and polished, and most have been expanded well beyond the restrictions imposed by magazine space and content limitations. The remaining stories are new and unpublished offerings written specifically for *Gun Dog Chronicles*.

Domestic dogs are human creations. Because their very existence lies in the context of their relationships with people, it follows that stories about hunting dogs must often encompass the hunters whose minds and hearts are bound to those animals. Thus, *Gun Dog Chronicles* includes pieces that—to a limited degree—explore mankind's emotional involvement in the lives of hunting dogs, as well as our vulnerability to their varied natures.

Not all of humankind's dealings with dogs are serious; neither are they always pleasant. There are moments of deep affection, humor, and even hilarity, mixed with equal rations of frustration, sadness, and—at times—despondency. Such is the nature of hunting-dog ownership; therefore, such are the pieces in this book.

You can read *Gun Dog Chronicles* however it pleases you: in order from beginning to end, or a story here, a story there—depending on your mood at the moment. Although each piece is independent of the others, they are linked by a common ingredient—a celebration of upland bird dogs and waterfowl retrievers.

Acknowledgments

Tales of experiences with hunting dogs aren't generated in the backyard. They require time out-of-doors, travel, diverse destinations, game birds, decent dogs when you get where you are going, and, later, the means to share these tales. In that vein alone, *Gun Dog Chronicles* owes much to many people.

Without the gracious professionalism of outfitters and gun-dog trainers across the country, my range of experiences afield would have been curtailed. I also owe thanks to the magazine editors who assigned me coveted regular columns and periodic features, then gently fostered their production by allowing me free rein to go where my mind directed.

Also critical were my bird-hunting companions over a wealth of seasons. Thanks for sharing your insights, your ideas, your dogs, yourselves. Above all, thanks for the memories of high times.

I offer my gratitude to Chris Cornell, my editor at Down East Books, for suggesting that I write *Gun Dog Chronicles*, for promoting it up the publishing chain-of-command, and for ramrodding the laborious process of turning what I gave him into a publishable manuscript. Aside from his editorial talents, Chris is a friend, a hunting partner, and a "dog man" of no mean skill.

My wife, Kathy, a partner in life and for life, has been with me every step of the way. Without her endurance, tolerance, and encouragement to "go for it"—whatever it was and wherever it took place—much of what is in this book, quite likely the book itself, and possibly even my writing career would not have become reality. I can't repay a debt of such magnitude. All I can say here is, "Thanks for being who and what you are." If I haven't made the rest clear by now, shame on me.

The gun dogs in my life and in this book would not understand the importance of the roles they've played over many seasons of change. That they will never know their significance is of no consequence. What matters is that I understand, that I know the value of what they have given me, and that I freely acknowledge every bit of it.

Introduction

The association between man and dog is unique, without parallel over the spectrum of our history. When we look at the human creation called dog, we open a window into our shadowy past, into ourselves and our present motivations, and—if we look closely—into the needs of our very souls. Indeed, no other animal begins to approach the domestic dog's involvement with us. It is equally certain that this personal and cooperative relationship has reached its zenith in hunters and their gun dogs. But this particular partnership goes deeper than the practical. If such complex terrain has true and enduring meaning, that meaning is found more in the heart than in the mind. Let me introduce *Gun Dog Chronicles* from that angle.

In today's world, there is little demand for livestock that simply toils for the benefit of man. Conversely, there is a powerful need for animals that share and uplift our sport, our pleasure, our sadness, and the emotional material of our lives, animals that require nothing in return for their giving but a modicum of our time and affection. Among the Earth's creatures, dogs alone can adequately fill this remarkable vacancy in the human heart.

And that is the theme of this book: the wonderment, the incomparable highs, and the sometimes desperate lows of gun-dog ownership. Here, too, are the unique events—along with the little, everyday things—that make our dogs what they are and, when taken together, coalesce into the grand alliance of hunter and dog.

It is little things like puppy breath or a first, tentative lick full of trust and promise that say so much, that bond us so firmly over a lifetime. Or it could be those lovely, almost para-lyzing moments when a dog's eyes are full of us and nothing else. Or it may be those October mornings when the presence of a dog transforms a landscape from completely beautiful to beautifully complete and elevates a shooting sport into an art form. It is little things, to be sure: a perfect woodcock feather stuck on a pointer's lip, fluttering lightly with the whisper of his breath; marsh ooze, ripe and fusty, but oddly fitting when caked on a retriever; a burr-matted ear that instantly responds to our touch and soft words.

Don't look for solutions in this book. I, too, have more questions than answers. Don't seek dispassion, detachment, or objectivity. When it comes to dogs, I offer none of those things. If *Gun Dog Chronicles* represents anything to you, let it be inti-mate sketches of the outdoor fabric, with gun dogs as both woof and warp of that fabric's weave. Allow me, if you will, to be an interpreter of autumn dreams, a messenger of days in bird covers and duck blinds, a visionary of great dogs and an apolo-gist for the mediocre—a representative of Everyman.

Think of me not as an expert at anything, but as someone who knows the merest bit about this and that. Label me as a person whose hands are better fitted for gripping a shotgun than a golf club, whose fingers feel more at home stroking a dog than a computer keyboard, whose palate is rough enough to thrive on rat cheese and cold beer. Sum me up as an un-abashed leaner against trees, a haunter of old homesteads with orchards of gnarled apple trees and ruffed grouse. Know me as one who loves worn canvas jackets; crows fussing like fish-wives; nights with good company, owl talk, and the wingtip etchings of bats; and days spent following dogs. Always dogs: they are the knot in the threads that tie me to the out-of-doors, an unbreakable knot cinched by the seasons and burnished by the flow of time.

Allow me, now, a moment to turn inward for personal reckoning.

The remembrance of things past often plays me false. Dim mind's-eye visions garnered from deep history and glossed by time tend to put a rosy hue on recollection. Given that, the first gun-dog memory that I can recapture with certainty involves a gray-muzzled, rheumy-eyed English pointer named Duke, who spent his well-earned retirement edged up to a fireplace. Duke belonged to my uncle, who would become my mentor in seasons ahead and was a feature player in fostering my love of hunting dogs.

Years later, my parents told me that as a youngster I spent hours snuggled on a hearth rug with that arthritic, bad-smelling old pointer. Now, all I have left is a time-shaded vignette of rubbing Duke's scarred head and staring into his eyes, utterly absorbed by their tranquillity and my vague self-image in the convex mirror of their surface. But this soft and haunting vision of Duke fills only a flash in time.

The true beginning of my gun-dog memories open with color: English-setter white muscle-bunched into a point on a golden day in woods dominated by crimson and the fleeting blur of woodcock brown. The memories are also of sound: my uncle's barely heard, "Easy now," to the dog or to me; a twittering whisper of flight; the background roar of my 16-gauge; the setter's name called for the retrieve. Then, there was the extraordinary sight of a dog presenting me with my first woodcock. I was a boy, and I was stunned by what I had seen.

"Put out your hand, and she'll give you the bird," my uncle told me. A smile flirted with the angular planes of his face.

"Go ahead," he urged, "take your bird."

I was overwhelmed not by the woodcock itself or by the death that I had caused, though I was aware of both. My mind had been dazzled by the living, moving beauty of the mellow-eyed setter in front of me waiting to complete the ritual of delivery.

"Dogs get in your blood fast, don't they?" my uncle asked, once I stopped gawking at the dog and took the surprisingly small handful of feathers she was offering. "I told you they would."

I had been around gun dogs since I graduated into long pants, in large part tagging along with my uncle while he trained and hunted his homegrown setters and the occasional pointer. But it took a real hunt with a white dog as its center-piece to focus and lock the magnitude of the drama into my juvenile brain.

"Dogs are why most of us bird hunt," my uncle said, adding emphatically, "You'll see it that way too, if I have anything to say about it."

Hunting really isn't about birds. Not at its heart. If game bagged is the sole measure of success, upland bird and water-fowl hunting are reduced from high sport to rather low business. It is even less about guns and loads and ballistics. Those are tools. Mostly, hunting is about dogs: pointers, flushers, and retrievers, whether big runners or close workers, high-nosers or ground snuffers. It is about chiseled heads and high tails, broad chests heaving from long retrieves, and flanks quivering after driving flushes. It is about looks from eyes burning with the fire of intense moments.

My uncle was right all those seasons ago: Dogs get in your blood. Across the years, the hand of fate has blessed me with some decent ones—day-in, day-out partners built of loyalty and an unquenchable desire for birds, matched with the ability to produce them. Typically, if there was shortchanging in these partnerships it came from my side at the expense of the dogs. Yet, they remained devoted and tolerant of my too-numerous faults, which gives credence to the old saw, "Love is like the morning dew; it's just as apt to fall on a horse turd as on a rose." To be sure, a lifetime of loving dogs bears witness to the "morning dew" quality of their affections.

A special few of these gun dogs guided me onto new pathways of action and thought, and—by their uniqueness—to higher levels of admiration and emotion. Others were just dogs, sound of character and fair-to-middling in performance. Still others led me on less-than-merry chases, both literally and figuratively. But without all of them—from Duke, my uncle's ancient pointer, to a white setter on a golden day, to the spaniels resting beside me now—my enthusiasm for walking life's road would have been diminished and the road itself less well traveled.

When I was a shirttail kid roaming the woods and fields and marshes with an array of dogs, I believed that if I ranged far and hunted hard I would find something truly wonderful. Those first partners departed along with my youth, but I know now that I already had that "truly wonderful" something and have had it many times since, in many ways, with the dogs I have followed.

And I intend to keep following gun dogs—those of yesterday, those of today, and those that might come tomorrow. And I hope that you will come along and follow some of them with me, here, among the words of *Gun Dog Chronicles*.

Joe Arnette
The "Bear's Den"
Kennebunkport, Maine

Part I

The Early Years

Happiness is a warm puppy.

—Charles Schulz

1
Breathing Room

Jesse, a five-year old English pointer, paced the cool floor of her kennel. Her movements, though regular and ritualized, had no purpose beyond helping her cope with a restless anxiety that was vaguely familiar but was something she could neither ease nor understand. She was not entering new territory, yet she responded to the insistent, hormonally-driven tensions exactly as she had with her previous two litters.

The dog moved into a shaded corner and smelled and pawed the floor, as though halfheartedly rearranging the concrete. She made several circles, then sprawled awkwardly on her side with her head and legs stretched, and her swollen belly sagging against the floor. She panted heavily, her tongue lolling over her lower jaw, and from time-to-time she lifted her head to nose and lick her distended body.

Soon, she was up and pacing to another spot to paw and sniff and sprawl again. Jesse could find no comfort; there was none to find. There were no means for her to calm her agitation or to relax a relentless, increasingly imminent urge. When the time came—and that time was close—nature would take control and, once again, guide her through the largely instinctual process of delivering her pups.

From a distance, the breeder watched Jesse with a practiced eye that accurately judged what was taking place. He was certain that her pups would come within twelve hours, which meant a sleepless night for both of them. Normally, during early-morning whelpings—which seemed to account for most of them—he had an assistant stay with the females, calling him only to deal with emergencies.

But Jesse was one of his personal gun dogs; she was special to him, as were the pups on the edge of arrival. This was a repeat breeding, and if these puppies turned out to be as fine as those from her first and second litters, he intended to keep one of them. That decision would come later; for now he had to make certain they entered the world with a minimum of struggle. He would be there if the dog needed him.

Jesse was predictable. It seemed, the breeder thought, as though she had read a textbook description of the classic way to produce puppies. She came into heat on schedule. Her other two litters had arrived exactly sixty-three days after breeding, and it appeared that this one would do the same. She had even had short bouts with morning sickness again. Three or four days before she was due, her ample, English-pointer appetite began to drop off—as usual—followed by restlessness and compulsive nesting behavior.

Just after dark, the breeder confined Jesse in the small whelping area off her kennel and run, as he had done each night for the past week. By now, she was accustomed to sleeping in the whelping box where she would bear her litter. She had water but no food; she had stopped eating a day-and-a-half earlier.

Three hours before daybreak, Jesse stretched full out on her side in the whelping box. She panted excessively, as though heat was a problem, then raised her head and vomited a small stream of fluid that the breeder quickly cleaned up. Jesse licked his hand as it passed in front of her muzzle. He stroked her head lightly, briefly, and moved back to his chair to watch from the darkened corner where he wouldn't disturb her. He would interfere only if something went wrong and the dog required his help.

The man did not enjoy seeing dogs give birth. He didn't view it as the much-described miracle of life, but as a natural and commonplace event. Occasionally, births were difficult and unpleasant, though typically they were little more than the final act in a complex two-month process that allowed dogs to reproduce more of their kind.

Part of what troubled him was the agitated confusion and apparent discomfort of whelping females, though he admitted to himself that the deliveries looked worse than they were. At birth, these pointer pups would be somewhat larger than good-sized chipmunks and thus not much of a problem for a healthy, sixty-pound dog. Experience and a logical mind told him these facts. Nonetheless, even after all of the whelpings that he had watched over two decades, his heart still went out to dogs that could not rationally interpret what was happening to them.

Mostly, it was the straining that got to the breeder, the straining that began moving pups into position for birth. It was the lifting of heads, the occasional, anxious whines, and the half-wild, disoriented looks flashing in the eyes. That's exactly what Jesse was going through now. He turned his head away, poured a cup of stale coffee that he didn't want, and began to flip, without interest, through the pages of a magazine. When he glanced at the dog again, he tossed down the magazine and spilled the coffee as he set the cup aside. The first pup was at the threshold of its birth.

Jesse's water had broken, and she passed a light-colored fluid. Within minutes, the pup's nose appeared, followed by a bit of its stubby muzzle and the tip of a front paw. The straining paused for a moment while Jesse panted and breathed in short bursts before beginning again to push out the remainder of the pup's head. There was a brief rest, and a final shove, then her puppy's body easily followed its head and was delivered onto the pad that covered the whelping-box floor.

The breeder watched closely, less tense now that the first pup was out, actually enthralled at this point as pure maternal instinct took charge. Jesse curved her body, bent her head to the rear, and immediately began to remove the amniotic sac that was still loosely cloaking the pup. She licked the small body vigorously, pulled the torn fetal membranes away, and shredded the umbilical cord with her teeth. No voluntary movement or sound had yet come from the newborn.

The nudging and licking went on as Jesse rough-cleaned the pup's muzzle and body, stimulating its blood to circulate and, especially, its lungs to begin working on their own. Then the tiny dog, less than a minute old, twitched several times, moved its legs, and cried out in a small, thin squeal.

The pup did not know that it had just performed the single most critical act of its entire life. No matter what happened in years ahead, it had accomplished the one thing that, above all others, would allow it to grow, develop, and—ultimately—to mature into what its considerable genetic potential suggested would be a fine dog. The pup had taken its first breath.

Jesse continued to clean it, to shift its position slightly, to nuzzle and smell it—all part of establishing that this pup was hers and of initiating the critical parent-offspring bond. When she relaxed for a moment and laid her head down, the breeder walked to the box and lifted the newborn into the cupped palm of his hand. It appeared to be a perfect male, with Jesse's all-white body, her rich liver head, and an identical creamy blaze running between its ears.

The pup squealed again, and Jesse looked nervously up at him. The man smiled as he bent down and snuggled the tiny white pointer close against the warmth of her belly and guided him onto a nipple. There was time enough for the pup to nurse before the next delivery. The pup would be fine, now that he had breathing room.

2
Pick of the Litter

"Which one do you like best, Dad?" the boy asked. With a twelve year old's, self-focused eagerness, he didn't wait for an answer. "I really like her," the boy added quickly, head gesturing down at the mostly white puppy in his arms. "She's the same one I picked the last time. See the spot on her head. And look. She likes me, too. I can tell."

"Yes, I think she does, son," the man said with mock seriousness, burying an indulgent smile as he watched the boy and the eight-week-old pointer go through the ritual, but by now needless, motions of choosing each other. In reality, there was nothing left to be worked out. The boy was a goner for the pup from the deciding moment when the delicate female ran to him, licked the hand he pushed forward and stared softly into his eyes.

What an amazing process, the man thought, though he had been through it himself many times. Occasionally, he had allowed logic to lead him in a choice of dogs, but mainly he had followed his heart. Just as his son was doing. Experience had taught him that it made sense, all other things in a litter being equal, to take the pup that couldn't leave him alone. He had rarely been disappointed when he had let young dogs do the picking.

"Let's put her down with the others," he told the boy, "and

watch what she does." The breeder, a family friend who had offered them pick of the litter, smiled at the boy's reluctance to give up the dog. He shrugged to affirm what the father already knew—that with such a fine litter, it didn't matter which pup the boy chose. And the breeder understood that it was, indeed, the boy's decision. The pup would be his first dog, his personal dog, not one of his father's.

Again on the ground with her littermates, the puppy did exactly what the boy's father hoped she would do—waddle around for a minute or so, check out what the other pups were doing, then race back to his son. She toyed briefly with his boot lace before putting her paws on his leg, scratching and yipping to be picked up. The boy turned his head to his father and presented him with a sunburst grin as big as the world. The light in his son's eyes took the man's breath away.

The boy dropped to his knees and let the puppy nibble his nose and lick his face, then he stretched out on the ground. The little pointer scrambled onto his belly, tugged at a fold of his shirt and play-growled at the strange, white buttons. She moved wobbly-slow up the uneven terrain of his chest until she reached his neck, where she wrapped herself into the warm hollow of his throat. The boy laid his smallish hand on the soft texture of her back and let it rest there. The eyelids of the boy and the puppy closed; both seemed content to remain how and where they were forever.

The other five pups had collected around the boy's feet in a mock battle with pant cuffs, boots, and each other's tails. Neither the boy nor his puppy cracked an eye or showed the slightest interest in the noisy affairs taking place. The boy had made his decision. He just hadn't said the words.

His father and the breeder-friend watched with an interest that went beyond a curiosity in the simple act of selection. The scene had an emotional depth that they both remembered—or thought they remembered—but could never recapture for themselves. Such impeccable purity was reserved for the young and, even then, only at special times. There were no cracks in the fineness of what the men saw. At that moment, boy and puppy were complete in themselves, with their mutual innocence frozen in time.

The man was enthralled. He could have watched his son until darkness shut him out, but in a low voice he said, "I guess you've made up your mind, but can you tell me why you want that pup more than the others?" His son's eyes didn't open. Nor did he speak immediately, as though he was stretching out and holding onto his feelings as long as he could, as though he understood they would not occur again with quite the same intensity.

"I don't know why, Dad," said the boy, after he stood. He looked down at the pup, and his hand began to stroke her back. "I just know that she's the one I want." He paused, searched his mind for a complex answer, but found only a simple fact: "She likes me. And I like her. Same as before, the first time we were here."

The man was pleased, content that his son had given him the truth as he saw it—or, more to the point, as he felt it. Beyond that, the man was gratified that the boy had found it unnecessary to justify or camouflage his love-at-first-sight for a puppy that ran to him purposefully, that choose him over littermates and play.

The boy seemed to have made his decision straight from the heart. And that was fine. But maybe there was more. He had been around his father's dogs all of his life, helped with their care since he was five, then graduated into greater responsibility for their training. Likely, he had learned more than was obvious and, though he couldn't articulate the exact reasons, had put what he knew into his choice.

On the other hand, the boy's father thought, maybe asking his son for a rational explanation was too much. The more he considered his question, the more it sounded foolish. He doubted that he could provide specific reasons for quite a few of his choices over the years—not at the least, reasons that made any degree of real sense.

The man was yanked from his thoughts when his son asked, hesitantly, as if afraid of hearing the answer, "You like her too, don't you, Dad? Don't you think she's the best?"

The father stepped close, put his hand on his son's thin shoulder, and said emphatically, to leave no doubt in the boy's mind, "Yes, I do, son. She's a fine pup. She's the one I would have picked for myself. What do you say we take her home?"

3
Sensing the
Possibilities

The English setter had known the world for eight weeks when she was plucked from her kennel and littermates by hands that were more hurried than rough. A voice spoke softly as the hands stroked her shoulders, inserted a needle, then massaged the vaccination site. The hands eased the pup into a small airline crate and secured the grated door. Crate and setter were lifted into a truck, which in turn delivered them to an airport terminal three hours away. Six hours later, the crate was carried into another terminal and placed on a special baggage shelf.

The setter lay curled and half-buried within tiers of shredded newspaper, staring out at a too-bright unknown that was broken into glittering squares by the crate's grill work. Long shadows and silhouettes passed through her field of vision. Clamor surrounded her. Then papers rustled on the crate's top, and a face appeared at the door, smiling at the sight of her. The face spoke words of no meaning to the puppy, gentle words whose purpose was to soothe and comfort. The door opened and a hand slipped slowly into the crate.

A few years ago, I picked up an English setter puppy for a friend. The timing of her arrival had caught him elsewhere, so I had the pleasure of the setter's company for the first week of her new life away from the security of all she had known. Now, some people might find "pleasure" to be a curious choice of words for a time measured in piles, puddles, and night-cries. And in a narrow sense, I wouldn't argue against their case. It would, indeed, take a strange person to extract joy from the by-products of good living that regularly lie waiting in puppy crates at six in the morning. But such events are a small part of a pup's presence.

Such inconveniences are pushed out of mind by the sights of an infant dog's initial contacts with its world. I mean those first days of exploration and discovery: the little victories of puppy courage over dark corners, rustling bushes, and threatening brushpiles; the temporary defeats as pine cones send the pup lopsidedly stumbling back to the safety of a pant leg. What's not to love in a young dog's assault on a wind-scurried leaf or in the insistent demands for playtime that are followed by a collapse into the comatose sleep known only to the very young. What's a little poop measured against the whole of a puppy?

A hand touched the setter's nose, lingered there for a moment before moving to smooth the ruffled, creamy fur under her chin. The hand stroked slowly down her side, across her rump and over her tail. Then, it withdrew back beyond the crate door. The puppy walked to the opening, thrust her head through it and stared out at a space foreign with towering shapes, noises she had never heard, and odors she had never smelled. One hand came again and cupped her rear, then another took her front and lifted her from the crate to the face with the smile and easy words.

Each pup is a new and individual experience. Each is different from those that have gone before and those that will come after. For some reason that I can't explain, this living uniqueness was hammered into me by my friend's little English setter, the one that wasn't mine. Perhaps it was simply my sense of responsibility for a pup temporarily in my care. More likely, I think, it was the immediacy of her visit, the fact that she belonged to someone else and that I wouldn't have the luxury of years—or even months—to know this dog that was thrust into my life. On the other hand, seven days is a delightfully long time when an eight-week-old youngster is taking tentative steps toward the possibilities in a new existence.

Time, as a concept, was meaningless to the setter. She was unaware of her past in any concrete sense, and had no anticipation of her future. Because she could not remember yesterday, she could not imagine tomorrow. She lived in the present, in a shifting world of immediate sensations where the possibilities were both nonexistent and endless. At this point in her life, her reality was the feel of the hands that cradled her securely. The details would come later.

I knew from her lineage that this setter had the makings of a first-class dog. Whether or not she lived up to that genetic potential remained to be seen, but from the beginning my guess was that she would deliver all that was expected from her. And why wouldn't she? Even for a puppy, the signs of style were there—still not formed, to be sure, but from her balanced head and body to an already high tail, it was clear that she came from a long line of winners.

Each time I looked closely at this setter, my mind hung up on a line by poet and dramatist John Dryden. The context of Dryden's work, and for that matter the work itself, had long departed my memory, but his words, "Of ancient race by birth, but nobler yet in his own worth," remained with me, only to be drawn out by the pup.

Her impressive pedigree aside, I liked the confidence in

her step and the curiosity in her expression. I liked the way she cocked her head at different angles when faced with a new sight or sound; the way she pushed out her dime-sized nose and flared her nostrils; the way she used all of her raw ability to sense the possibilities of the world she had entered but did not know. Most of all, I liked her eyes.

The face with the broad smile and easy words was inches away. She could smell breath, roughly similar to the few other breaths she had known, yet different in its makeup. Hands drew her close to the face, nearer now to the voice, which had fallen to a whisper. They then nestled her tightly against a warm neck and chest. Her nose pushed farther into the neck, smelled it, nuzzled it, licked it. Small tremors shivered across the little setter's body before the flap of a coat folded around all but her head. The large face looked down, close and straight into her eyes. The setter pup stared back. Her look was noncommittal but confident, more unfamiliar with the closeness of the eyes than afraid of them. A finger touched her, and the voice spoke again.

On the surface, her eyes appeared to be blank, brownish mirrors reflecting pieces of my own image. But below the surface, beyond my shadowy outline, the eyes were ancient, like those of the Earth's first dog. Within that puppy's eyes, there was a world as old as time, yet as new as its original moments. They were full of an undefinable essence—maybe an atavistic wisdom or the knowledge and trust of ages, perhaps an inherent sense of acceptance and fate. I'll never know, and I am not unhappy with that. Some mysteries are better left unexplored, and the first look into the depths of a puppy's eyes are one of them.

It's possible that I am making too much of those brief days with my friend's English setter pup. Maybe I was taken with her simply because she was there. It is certainly true that I never met a puppy I didn't like. But, whatever the reason, this dog who belonged to another made me think beyond her as an individual, beyond the necessities she required, and beyond myself as the provider of those necessities. She rattled me out of an established, functional mind-set and forced me to ponder the subtleties of abrupt shifts and stunning shocks. I had to look, too, at the emotional upheavals and elemental fears, the demands of acceptance, the adjustment and human expectation that confront each puppy in its moment-to-moment view of life.

The voice spoke again as she was carried to a truck, where she crawled from the coat onto a lap. She smelled the steering wheel, looked into a cup of cold coffee, nosed a box of shotgun shells, then seemed to come to a decision. Nine hours after she had been taken abruptly from all that was familiar and safe, the English setter puppy tucked herself deep into the lap, beneath the comforting protection of a warm hand, and slept a silent, dreamless sleep.

4
Warm Puppies

I was being mugged, and it was over in minutes. Like the other times, there was a struggle backed by throaty, assailant grumblings; tugged clothing; and thrashings on the ground. Then the theft was complete. I had no defense, and quickly lost my most precious possession. The muggers were warm puppies, thieves of hearts, and they had stolen mine with little effort.

I was lying on the midsummer earth, feeling its heat oozing up the stems of the low-cut meadow grass that prickled through my shirt. My face tingled with sunlight where it crept in below a hat brim, flashing tiny dots and speckled glitter across the inside of my eyelids. A chainsaw growled in a woodlot several fields away, while two hammers rhythmically tap-tapped nails nearby. Homing pigeons fluttered overhead in helter-skelter pursuit of their endless pigeon business.

The muggers closed in on me again. There were five of them in the gang, fanned out and on the prowl for action. I admit that I had tempted them and set myself up as an easy target—like a man walking down a mean street at midnight flashing $100 bills. Relishing my certain fate. I had stretched out on their puppy turf, wriggling a quail wing in the grass and making small tongue-popping noises.

One of the gang worried my pant leg; another thought my

boot sole had the most to offer; a third and fourth were on
my chest, rooting around for the wing now stuffed in my
shirt. The last, a smallish female, decided the mugging was
over and went to sleep in the V of my legs. She was right. I
had already lost all there was to lose. And they weren't even
my pups, nor did I intend to pick one out. It was simply playtime—social hour—at a friend's kennel. But when there is a
litter of warm puppies to steal your heart, who thinks about
ownership, about purpose, about breed or sex or color, about
anything but the happiness of the moment.

Charles Schulz could not have foreseen that the title of
his delightful 1962 book of cartoons, *Happiness Is a Warm
Puppy*, would become a byword. Schulz, of course, is the cre-
ator of the cartoon strip *Peanuts*; the much-put-upon, "round-
headed kid," Charlie Brown; and, most of all, that paragon of
pooches, Snoopy.

Somewhere, I suppose, there are swine who loathe puppies. I imagine them lurking in dark corners, robbing old
folks, and frightening children in their spare time. However,
to be fair about this, there are also quite decent people who,
for reasons unfathomable by most standards, don't give a tin-
ker's damn about anything with four legs. But for the rest of
us, in five words, a mere twenty-one letters, Charles Schulz
closed the kennel door on the subjects of happiness and warm
puppies.

Now I'm not a complete Pollyanna about puppies. It's true
that they can escape with my heart before it beats a half-dozen
times, but when pups dart off with a custom duck call or fly
rod or half of a high-end pair of boots, my heisted affections
will harden. Just a touch, mind you, and not for long—especially when they crawl up onto my neck, lick my cheek in con-
trition for offenses they don't yet understand, then lose their
heads and attack my mustache. In fact, I'm convinced that

when puppies come to live with me, their first learning experience—after pinpointing the food and toys—is, "I can get away with anything if I lick his face and chew his mustache."

How about those times when we doze on a couch and let our hand slide to the floor, waking to find a pup asleep with his head in our palm? Or when we snooze on the floor and he waddles over, curling—warm and clean and perfect—into the curve of our neck and shoulder? When such things happen, puppy transgressions dry up like a spattering of summer raindrops. Who remembers an accident on a rug or a piece of furniture pocked with tiny tooth marks when the cuddly culprit is murmuring comfort noises in our lap and staring up at us with sleep-heavy eyes that are deep, innocent wells waiting to be filled with love and a good life?

Other moments, too, remain sharp in memory. Moments of grass and water, wind and butterflies; of nervous, neck-stretched investigations of dark stumps; of bungling feet traveling in different directions at different speeds; of self-images not recognized in reflective rain puddles. A puppy is potential waiting to be realized, and each instant, each gust of breeze with its smells, each shadow with its possibilities and unknowns etches a new mark on the clean slate of his experience. Watching a youngster sample those instants, wind gusts, shadows, and reflections, is to see a life begin its emergence into the world. It is a tempered blend of fear, curiosity, and the push to know, always prompting the pup to look back over his shoulder to make certain we are still close and securely with him. Perhaps it is those looks—the quick glances that speak of an uncluttered need for us to be there—that are the best of such moments.

It was late autumn the last time I was mugged, during a grouse-hunting trip with a friend. He had a warm beauty of a puppy, an English pointer three months old and newly arrived at his kennel. He brought her along to ride in laps, nibble on fingers, smell new winds and learn—without effort—that life can be fun. Part of the socializing process was inviting her to bed down with her owner for the night. She proved very good at it.

Waking up in darkness paled by a strong moon beaming through a window, I glanced the few feet to my friend's bunk. Two heads were on the pillow—one large and mustachioed, the other small with its floppy, liver ears flipped back. Beneath the little head, a white paw rested outside the blanket. The thief of hearts struck again and I was helpless.

My friend did not know that I borrowed a few hours of contentment, that I eased the sleep-warm puppy from the covers and carried her to my bed, where she stayed folded into the crook of my arm until I returned her at dawn. Happiness and warm puppies? Just different words for the same thing.

5
Generations

"She looks good," I said to my uncle, gesturing casually toward the sparkling twelve-week-old setter pup nestled in his arms, "but will she hunt?"

That line, lifted from a bird-hunting book he had given to me, had appeared mature and quite professional in print. It seemed to suggest a true eye for dogs, backed by unplumbed depths of knowledge. But when I delivered those few words in my cracking, puberty-ravaged voice, they sounded as foolish as they really were.

My uncle thought so, too. He was a big man who seemed to swell even larger with indignation. His thick eyebrows crawled up his forehead like angry caterpillars before he leveled a fiery stare that shriveled my already troubled vocal cords.

"Will she hunt?" he repeated to himself, apparently dumbfounded by the question. His eyebrows were thrashing at the edge of his hairline. "Of course, she'll hunt," he growled in his clipped, northern accent. "Her bloodlines are better than yours—and mine—by a long shot." He pulled the pup a little closer to his chest, protectively, as though an evil spirit lurked nearby, then added, "I should know better than to give you books full of idiotic one-liners."

He then looked at me appraisingly and said, "You might

want to think about a career in writing. Anyone with a short attention span and an IQ the size of a dog collar should be pretty good at it." My uncle did not think highly of outdoor writers, especially when they dealt with the intricacies of working gun dogs. Little did he know the prophecy in his words.

The fuzzy caterpillars had returned to their resting habitat above his eyes when he put a peace-offering hand on my shoulder and felt around it for a moment, thoroughly, just as he checked the thriftiness of his dogs. "You need to eat more. You're nothing but bones." That said, he returned to his just-interrupted lecture on puppies—to my uncle, a far more important subject than his nephew's weight.

"Picking a puppy—even out of a litter like this one, from proven dogs—is always a gamble. It's experience and knowing the breeding, then going with intuition and hoping for some luck. I've bred generations of these setters, and I know what to expect from them. Still, I can't pinpoint what this pup shows me or explain why I think she's the best of the seven, maybe one of the best I've ever produced."

To my amateurish eyes, the other six puppies yipping, nipping, and gamboling around our feet looked nearly identical to the little female in my uncle's arms. "And my gut feeling about this dog might be way off base," he admitted. "Maybe I just like her for some reason I'll never understand. But one thing is certain," he emphasized, jamming a sausage-like finger at me and arrowing another stare directly into my eyes. "She will hunt.

"Anyway, right or wrong, this is a pup I'm going to keep," he said, rubbing the dog's side softly and moving the fingers of his other hand rhythmically under her chin. Her eyelids had drooped to half-closed "You can help me fool with her this summer if you like." I liked but wanted to start now.

"You know better than that," he said, glancing at me. "I've

told you a hundred times that pups need to have fun, a lot of
it, before they learn that life has a business side to it." Clearly,
she was my uncle's dog, and waiting until summer to "fool
with her" would have to be enough.

"What are you going to call her?" I asked, ready to volun-
teer my own heavy thoughts on a perfect handle for the pup.
"I haven't decided yet," he answered, "I need to think about it
a little more." My uncle was fussy about names for his dogs.
He wasn't the call-'em-anything-'cause-they-don't-care sort.
"Always give a dog a decent name," he had drilled into me,
"something short and fitting, but most of all, dignified.
There's nothing worse than a silly name on a serious dog."

He handed me the pup and said, "Here, hold this dog and
look at her closely. Look into her eyes and tell me she doesn't
deserve the best that I can give her, including the right name."

When I took that puppy into my arms and really saw her,
she became everything that was important. My world nar-
rowed, then focused tightly on a warm bundle of fur. There
was no yesterday, no tomorrow, not even a today, other than
the reality of a moment when sweet-smelling life snuggled into
my neck and licked my ear lobe. She was a Llewellin type,
white with smudges of auburn on her brows and muzzle, and a
silver-dollar-sized black spot on her rump. She would grow to
medium build but stay fine-boned and on the light side, the
way my uncle liked his setters. At three years, she would be an
all-day dog—fast and agile, with an economy of movement.

But none of that mattered to me. She was perfect the way
she was: soft as a June morning between my hands, her heart
beating against my chest, her breath fresh as newly baked
bread. The pup's eyes were deep and full of questions, but—
like mine too young to have any answers. Mostly, her look
was full of trust. Maybe the eyes were what told my uncle to
keep this puppy.

"She's beautiful," I said, the snappy one-liners and adolescent, octave-skipping voice forgotten. There was nothing in my head but an overwhelming desire for that setter. I had been around quite a few dogs in my short life, but I wanted that particular puppy more than any other I'd seen. I wanted her more than Christmases, birthdays, girlfriends, and a deep voice put together.

"You'll have one like her someday," my uncle assured me, smiling as if he had peered into my mind, his Yankee gruffness melted at the sight of a suddenly vulnerable, shiny-eyed kid holding a puppy. "Down the road, I'll see to it that you get a nice dog from this line—that is, if you learn enough between now and then. I'll start you and the pup, both, this summer."

How much I learned over the years was debatable, but my uncle's word remained good. Although it took a while, he did indeed see to it that I got a "nice dog," a very nice dog, from his generations of setters. His gut feeling about the stunning Llewellin pup I had held as a boy was borne out beyond his hopes: As it would with her great-great-granddaughter— auburn brows and inky spot intact—who fourteen years later was again the world snuggled into my neck, who licked my earlobe and flooded my nose with breath that still smelled like fresh bread.

6

Generations Revisited
—The Gift

The puppy arrived on my birthday by chance alone. My uncle wasn't the emotionally frivolous sort, and I knew for a fact that it wouldn't have occurred to him to send the pup as a gift on that particular day. In his mind, a fine gun dog was a treasure at any time; a special occasion wasn't necessary. I knew, as well, that he couldn't remember my birthday any more than he could pinpoint his own without considerable thought. The eight-week-old English setter was ready to go—it was that simple—and I was ready for her. That, at least, was my uncle's hope.

He warned me over the phone the night before he put her on a plane, "If you don't do right by this dog, I'm going to come out there and snatch you bald-headed." My uncle had heard that gem during one of his deep-south quail hunting trips and had used it effectively for years. He'd been threatening to remove my hair since I was a finger-in-nose kid, and he had come close a time or two when I had done something stupid around his dogs. He still thought of me as a goofy twelve year old. How he figured on knowing what the pup and I were doing from more than twenty-five hundred miles away was beyond me. "I have connections you don't know about," was all he'd say. And he might very well have had his big fingers tapped into some national network of dog-sorts that I had no clue about. Not that his connections mattered. I had waited fourteen years for this setter, and I intended to do as right by her as I could.

"She's a sweetheart of a pup," he said with a softening of his sharp accent. "Treat her like a lady, train her the way I taught you, and she'll be as fine a dog as you'll ever own." My uncle had the social niceties of a wild hog with sore teeth, but he thought of his dogs as ladies and gentlemen. "You be at the airport when she gets there," he ordered. "Don't make her wait." That finished the talk.

She was out of her crate, loose on the airport's loading dock, when I arrived. Stiff, oddball winds had blown her plane in unpredictably early. Nonetheless, close to a continent away, I could sense my uncle gnashing his teeth. My scalp prickled from long-distance fingers snatching at my hair. But the puppy was having a grand time with four burly, rough-looking dock workers—all down on their knees playing with her, slipping her sandwich bits, and cooing baby talk to the white, bright-eyed package of fur skittering over the floor.

"We just wanted to make sure she was all right," one of the men said hesitantly, in a semi-guilty tone, as if he'd been caught in an embarrassing but not quite wicked act. Another worker, who was more up-front, walked to me cradling the dog in his arms and apologized, "Sorry we let her out, but I just had to hold her. This is the prettiest puppy I've ever seen." I understood exactly what he meant when he handed her to me and said, "I'd give most anything to have a dog like this."

Years slid away as if time had reversed itself. I was an awestruck kid again, holding this pup's great-great-grandmother against my neck and wanting her more than anything, hearing my uncle say, "You'll have one like her someday. I'll see to it that you get a nice dog from this line."

Then time flipped back again and that "nice dog," the singular birthday gift that my uncle did not know he'd given me, was snuggled asleep in my lap, headed to her new home. I couldn't stop looking at her. She was elegant in her own right, yet as familiar to me as an old wish; the resemblance to what my mind's eye remembered of her great-great-grandmother was eerie. I did, indeed, have "one like her," just like her, complete with face markings and the black, silver-dollar-sized rump spot.

But even in my truck, with the setter pup now mine, my uncle's voice tracked me like a big-nosed hound. "Never let a dog ride free in a vehicle," he harped at me from the past. "You could have an accident, and the dog might get hurt." To my uncle, people figured into accidents only as the fools who let them happen. Although he was right about free-riding dogs and although his "connections you don't know" hovered in the back of my mind, the pup stayed warm-curled and travel-exhausted on my legs. I drove slowly and defensively, with one eye on the road, the other on the setter, and a happy little boy's birthday smile on my face.

"How's she doing?" my uncle asked without preliminaries during one of his numerous—and pesky—phone calls over the weeks after the puppy arrived. "You'd better be treating her right or—" I interrupted and finished his familiar words, "or you'll snatch me baldheaded." He was worse than the doting, overprotective father of a virginal daughter. "Don't worry," I reassured him, "she's doing fine; actually, better than fine." I told him what had happened two days before.

The sky was blue-clear, the earth dew-moist. It was one of those clean mornings when the air wasn't yet hot enough to lean on you. The pup was frisking along the edge of a marsh in a fallow wheat field, getting out more than I expected, scattering sparrows, chasing butterflies, smelling mouse nests. She was just having fun, I explained to my uncle before he could jump me about starting her too soon.

Suddenly, she stopped in midstride as if she had bumped into a glass wall. Taking a couple of wobbly, uncertain steps to one side, she then hoisted her tail and froze. I thought she was sight-pointing the butterfly ahead of her until it fluttered off unnoticed. Moments later, a cock pheasant, caught in short weeds, squawked up fifteen feet from her flared mini-nostrils. She stayed put at the flush, stared hard at the flying bird for a few seconds, then lined to where the rooster had crouched and rammed her nose deep into the narcotic scent. Another little boy's grin spread wide before I turned, looked far toward the northeast, and whispered, "Thank you."

"It won't always be that easy," my uncle said when I finished gloating, "but I've been telling you for years that you don't have to teach a well-bred English setter to point. I know you've had a bunch of dogs since we were together, but you haven't had setters—at least not one like this pup. Just take it slow, and use your head with her.

"By the way," he added in his abrupt, conversation-over, fashion, "next bird season, I'll be out to hunt with you—and to check on the dog." He never made it, but his gift of generations did. I think he would have liked her.

7

Lemon

Life is full of regrets, those errors of judgment that a friend of mine labeled "should-haves": I should have done this, I should have gone there, I should have taken that risk. Although a good many of my personal should-haves are little more than vague recollections of things past, fanciful thoughts, or wishes gone by, a few transcend such simple dreams. One, in particular, haunts me still and comes to the fore when aspens yellow and woodcock fly.

I should have bought Lemon; I really should have. Letting her get away from me was a blunder that I allowed to happen. And I still don't know why, not fully.

It was midway through an October of more than passing beauty. But the upland splendor was deceptive and incomplete. Grouse were down in numbers, and woodcock were—at best—average; both were scattered. A spring of cold rains had nipped the broods of the two species, and it had been followed by a summer, then an autumn, of severe drought that forced woodcock to the margins. It was a hot, hard season for hunters and dogs alike—a time when each bird was earned.

My retriever was sprawled and cooling in the shallows of a river oxbow when a man walked from the woods and followed the riverbank to where I stood. A small English pointer heeled solidly at his knee; it stopped when he stopped and waited for his command. The man bent slightly at the waist and stroked the dog's head, then, in a voice so low I barely heard it, said, "Okay." The pointer joined my dog in the water.

We passed the normal hunter pleasantries. We talked about the rains, the drought, the unseasonable autumn heat, and—of course—birds and dogs. We discovered that we lived less than twenty-five miles apart, that we had acquaintances in common, and that we had both hunted this covert for several years. During the conversation, the man's pointer left the water, shook, and trotted to his side. Again, the hunter gave his command in a near-whisper: "Down." He squatted next to the dog and ran his hand slowly along her back. As he knelt, I noticed a bit of bulge in his game vest and saw the protruding tip of a grouse tail.

"We worked some birds," he said casually, answering my question. "Three grouse and seven woodcock. I shot one of each; that's enough, given these conditions." I was surprised; perhaps astonished is the better word. My dog was a trained and experienced flushing retriever—a competent upland dog by any standard—but I hadn't seen ten birds in three days of hunting. And, it wasn't yet midmorning. That's when I took a closer look at the man's dog.

With one exception, her appearance was that of a typical, nicely proportioned English pointer. She had a lean, well-muscled body topped by a small head with chiseled lines and high-set, lemon-hued ears. Her main color was a rich, creamy white with tiny specks of the same lemon hue dusting her shoulders. Her eyes were soft, alert, and strikingly attentive. But the thing that stood out about her was her size: she was roughly the height of a small springer spaniel, and I guessed her weight at under thirty-five pounds—soaking wet, after a huge meal.

"She's small and doesn't look like anything in particular," the man said in a slightly defensive tone as he watched my appraisal, "but Lemon's a wonderful dog. She's by far the best all-around pointer I've ever owned and maybe—even at her age—the finest I've ever seen. She's not quite two years old—technically still a pup."

He paused, as though he was deciding how much to tell a complete stranger. Then he said suddenly, "I'm sick because I can't keep her." His voice seemed to droop as he told me that he had been transferred to a European urban center and was leaving in less than two weeks.

"It's impossible for Lemon to go with me," he explained. "And I need cash to settle a pressing issue, so I have to sell her. Otherwise, I'd give her to the right person. I'm looking for someone who will keep up her training, hunt her regularly, and provide her with the kind of home she deserves."

He paused again and stared down at the resting dog, then added, "I've already offered her to two close friends. Both of them admit that Lemon is one of the nicest dogs of any age they've shot over, but neither can get past what they call her 'problem.' To them, her size means she has no staying power and can't cover enough ground. They're wrong on both counts."

For a while, the man and I talked about larger gun dogs. I told him that I put no more stock in the virtues of a hefty build than he did, that to me—allowing for talent and athletic skills—the size of a dog's heart was more important than the size of its body. He nodded in agreement.

Then he stared at me in an odd, sidelong way and said, "This weather is too hot for a retriever." As if emphasizing his words, he removed his hat and used it to wipe a sheen of sweat from his forehead. "Why don't you put your dog on lead and come with us. Maybe Lemon can find a bird or two."

The next hour was a clinic, not in gun-dog handling—the man didn't say three words to the pointer—but in pure bird work. Lemon found four woodcock in an area that I had washed out, and she pinned each with stylish finesse. She patterned perfectly for the cover—close and cautious where necessary, then wide and fast where range was called for. Lemon was completely steady to wing and shot, and she retrieved to hand.

"She'll flush and resteady if you want her to," the man said at one of her points. She did, and without an unnecessary step.

He invited me to join him the following day in a big grouse covert that I knew was challenging even in a normal year. It was cover I wouldn't have hunted in such hot weather. But in an hour and a half, before the heat got too heavy, Lemon worked and rigidly pointed a half-dozen birds. "Impressive" is too weak a word for each of her performances, but one piece of bird work—the last of the morning—remains etched in my mind's eye as the defining memory of Lemon.

We had just finished hunting a steep, down-sloping clearcut that was machine-rutted, piled with slash, and tangled with regrowth. I thought that if Lemon's size was ever going to be a liability, it would show on this rough and broken terrain. She put that concern to rest by barely breaking stride on the gouged earth and by slipping effortlessly through the slash.

The clearcut ended abruptly where it bumped against a long alder run at the slope's bottom. A wide stand of pines rose high beyond the run. The man and I could hear Lemon's bell as she curled into the alders, seeking a feel for what little ground breeze there was. Lemon's owner cocked his head as the bell fell silent, almost immediately began tinkling again, then stopped once more.

"She's in the pines now, on a moving grouse," he said. "Let's go. She's waiting for us." The man bulled through the alders toward the stand of conifers, angling to the right of where the bell had sounded. I shifted to the left. I had no idea what he meant by "She's waiting for us."

The pines were dense and interwoven, but the limbs on the first five feet of each trunk had died back, offering a clear view of the stand's floor. I knelt low and saw the man, also kneeling, off to my right. Lemon was about thirty yards ahead, standing loose in what looked to be a soft, uncertain point—not at all the style I had watched earlier.

The man made a small, peeping lip-whistle. Lemon glanced sideways and saw him, then shook her head slightly and tinkled her bell. I realized that she was sounding her location. The man signaled me to stay put and dropped his hand in a chopping motion. Lemon broke from her stand and sprinted away for perhaps another forty yards before her bell indicated that she was looping back toward us. The pointer had gotten ahead of the running grouse and had cut off its escape.

When the bell stopped, the man lip-whistled again; the bell tinkled again. He signaled me to move ahead. Then we saw Lemon in front of us: tail high, shoulders and head low, body locked in a straight plane and leaning hard toward a dead pine toppled at the edge of a small, sunny glade. I was directly across the blowdown from Lemon when the man held up his hand and motioned me to get ready. He eased a few yards closer to the dog, then snapped his fingers and swung his arm forward.

Lemon launched herself into the pine limbs and nearly out the other side, the grouse flushing through sunbeams just feet from her nose. The moment the bird was airborne, the dog stopped dead still—one hind leg was still in the cluster of limbs—and marked the flight and feathery tumble until the man spoke her name. Her retrieve of the savvy cock grouse was as true and unblemished as the rest of her performance.

The man smiled broadly at Lemon, then turned to me and said, "We won't do better than that; besides, it's getting hot. How about calling it a morning?" I could only nod in a way that meant I had no words for what I had just witnessed.

Back at his truck, as the three of us sat on the tailgate, the man handed me a cup of coffee and asked if I'd like to buy Lemon. His price was high but fair, given the dog and the work he had obviously put into her. The offer didn't surprise me; I had an inkling that he might make it after inviting me to see her in action a second time. I guessed that not only was I there to judge Lemon, but I was being judged, as well. I had indecisively batted around thoughts of owning the diminutive pointer most of the previous night.

"You won't find a better dog than Lemon," he said bluntly, putting his arm around her shoulders. The pointer licked his face, then curled between us. She rested her head on my leg and closed her eyes. The man looked down at her as he continued. "I admit that she's not finished and needs experience"—he listed a few minor flaws in her bird work—"but even as a youngster she'll give you a quality hunt you can't expect from many dogs." He saw me lightly fingering her lemon ear and added, "But I think you understand what she has to offer."

The man slowly turned his head and stared down the line of sharply crimson maples fringing the logging road where we were parked. When he shifted back to me, his tone was soft and distracted, as if he was talking to himself. "What she did yesterday and today is Lemon, pure and simple; there are no surprises. She'll only get better. And she's a perfect lady around the house."

I believed the man completely, though I had hunted behind his dog just twice. I told him that to my eye Lemon's shortcomings were practically nonexistent, that she was a joy to watch, and that—regardless of her youth and her size—she was the most stunning pointer I had hunted behind in quite a few years. Nonetheless, as I had done the night before, I hedged on buying her.

I mentioned to him again that I already had three retrievers. I explained, in some depth, that I was committed to flushers and was by no means sure I could fit a pointing dog into my life, even one like Lemon. Or, perhaps, especially one like her, adding the qualifier as an afterthought without knowing exactly what I meant.

We agreed that he'd call me the next night for my decision. But at that moment, without saying the words, I think we both knew what the decision would be.

I should have bought Lemon; I really should have. To this day, I haven't come to grips with why my mind balked at the chance to own that singular dog, when my heart leaped at thoughts of her. Maybe, in part, it was a money concern—the man wasn't giving her away. Maybe it was wanting to avoid the hassle of taking on a fourth dog at the wrong time. Maybe it was realizing that my days were already far too full to do the pointer justice. More likely, though, it was the reverse of doing her justice—the worrisome gut knowledge that Lemon would become too important to me, that I would focus on her to the point of neglecting other facets of my life, particularly my retrievers.

A year or so later, a perceptive friend fine-tuned my nagging, undefined regrets about Lemon by implying that perhaps—for a number of reasons—I had been unconsciously afraid to own a dog of her caliber. He suggested that at certain times, very special dogs are better left to live in the mind alone.

Whatever the actual truth of the matter, there are few October days when I don't have visions of a too-small, creamy white English pointer flowing through cover like a wisp of smoke.

Oh yes, I still dream of Lemon when aspens yellow and woodcock fly.

8
Dreamin'
Perfection

Dirty woolen clouds scudded low over the man and his spaniel. Scattered raindrops, the remnants of a wind-driven night storm, tap danced on the wet earth around them. In the distance, thin blades of sun knifed through the breaking clouds and shimmered on the rain-beaded grass that topped the coulees well in front of the man and the dog. Altogether, it was a fine morning for a pheasant hunt, but the man sat where he was, reluctant to cut the springer loose and move out after birds.

"What's it going to be this time?" he asked the fidgeting dog. "Another day like the last few, or are you going to do your job?" At the low voice, the springer pulled his eyes off the horizon, turned his head and laid it on the man's leg. His half-tail swept arcs in the grass, while his sloe-eyed look angled up until it met the man's downward stare. The dog had bright, captivating eyes with something at home behind them, but the man wondered if he would ever discover the essence of that something.

Years before, an old-time trainer who seemed to have a straight track into gun-dog heads had told him, "It's in their eyes. Pay attention to their eyes, study them, and you'll know what a dog has to give you." If that was true, the man had thought early on, this springer should have it all. But knowing eyes aside, his dog hadn't put the game together. He didn't have it yet, whatever it was.

The man stroked the dog's finely-cut head, then stood and heeled him a few yards before releasing him with a finger-snap and a clipped, "Okay." He slid shells into the shotgun's twin tubes, snapped them closed, and whispered—more to the running clouds than the sprinting dog—"Let's see what you've got today." For nearly two years, he had expected perfection: Now he was prepared for nothing.

*   *   *

The puppy had seemed flawless from the beginning, when it poked a cautious nose out of the airline crate to sniff the man's outstretched hand, then bent its neck backward to focus on the face looming above. Grinning down at the beautiful bundle of fur nuzzling his fingers, he thought of the old-timer's words, "It's in the eyes," and looked hard for the future. But all he saw were pinpoints of light reflected at him from the rich spaniel eyes. "Maybe later," he said to the little male as he nestled the dog into his shirt collar, "when they've got more to tell me."

At a year, they told him a lot. The pup was a trainer's delight, with no balkiness or belligerence, and he had a temperament that was neither submissive nor dominant, but an ideal blend of independence and spirited cooperation. The man was building a long-term partnership, teaching the pup house rules when he was inside, kennel rules when he was not, and obedience wherever he was. Mainly, he taught the pup love and fun. He was taking it slow and easy, thinking about everything he did, trying not to repeat mistakes he had made on other dogs. The man had a clear picture of what he wanted from this springer, and he wasn't going to lose it by pushing too hard, too fast.

"Let me see you run," he said to the happy-eyed pup when he turned the dog loose after short work sessions. The leggy, white youngster with the liver ears and rump-splotch flowed like a ground breeze, like the man's dream of perfection—head up, dropping the nose he never outran only when he struck hot scent. From the first, the dog moved with a fluid grace that would surely transfer its style to the hunting patterns the man would later drill into him.

He did not have to teach the young spaniel the meaning of game. The pup was born with birds seared into his brain. For six months, the man kept the brain-flame roaring, fueled by pick-ups, flushes, and free-chases of planted pigeons. Then came gunfire, more pigeons, pen-raised pheasants, and longer, marked retrieves. During his first autumn, the pup met wild birds and dealt with them as if they were old friends.

At close to two years, however, the dog's eyes had less to say. A desire for birds, enthusiasm, and an increasingly polished style were there in abundance. The pup had accepted control with no more than minor glitches. The problem was that the dog's learning curve had frozen at around fifteen to sixteen months. From that point on, nothing changed. The spaniel neither backslid nor advanced. He had picked up the individual threads of hunting with ease; then, however, when he should have been knitting those threads into an ever-tightening weave, the pup hit a wall. The lack of consistency in the springer's successes and mistakes told the man that his training wasn't unraveling; it had never come fully together.

For several days, the dog would run perfect patterns, even when faced with more complex wind conditions. Forty-eight hours later, during a simple quartering drill, he would be all over a half-section. On one bird, he would be steady to flush but would break at the shot, while on the next he would re-verse himself. On identical retrieves, he would make a fast, clean, pick-up, then miss the next mark by twenty yards.

After a year's work beyond the basics, the springer had yet to link each of the elements in a hunt—finding, flushing, and fetching a bird—together into a complete chain without losing it at some point. The man's dream of perfection had become a nightmare of frustration.

"A dog will come into its own on its own schedule," was another piece of wisdom the old-timer had given him. "None of them are the same, and you shouldn't force what isn't there yet. If you've trained the right way, a good pup will put it together. Maybe not when you think he should, but sooner or later. And, as often as not, it will happen when you don't expect it. It pays to cut a young dog some slack."

By the second week of the spaniel's second season, the man had run out of slack to cut his pup. Perhaps the old-timer had been wrong and a dog's eyes were nothing more than a way to see the world—not windows into its heart. As he watched the springer make a slashing cut through the wet grass, the man thought that perhaps he had read deep meaning into eyes that showed simple affection.

*   *   *

A breeze fluttered down out of the shredding clouds and rumpled the grassland. The quartering dog caught the light wind and angled slightly to work it head-on. Within fifty yards he made game; his tail windmilled, and his head dropped to work the ground for foot scent. As the man moved up, the dog took off on a running pheasant's hot, twisting track, heading toward a wide drainage ditch that was thick with swampy growth.

"Too far out," the man muttered to himself. He blew a sharp blast on the whistle to stop the dog, forgetting that he couldn't enforce the command. But the springer bounced and slid into a half-sit—wide-eyed and up on his toes—and waited for the man to catch up. A finger snap sent him off, with the man staying close behind. At the edge of the ditch, the dog lost the trail, made a sweep back into the grass, found it again, and ran it into the weed-choked bottom.

The rooster jumped, with the spaniel airborne and neck-stretched behind him, grabbing for tail feathers. It was a hard flush that hooked the bird to the side, well away from the man. Out of habit, the man glanced toward the dog, who had hit the ground sitting, before he pulled down on the rooster and crumpled it into the waving grass. He marked the bird down, then turned to look for the springer, who he expected to see anywhere but where the dog was—half-hidden by weeds but still hupped, butt-down, at the point of the flush.

The man held his breath and said nothing for a moment; he let the spaniel sit, still focused on the bird's hooking flight line. At his name, the dog rocketed out of the ditch. When he narrowly missed the bird on his first cast, he stopped and looked back at his owner. "This one is all yours," the man said in a voice as quiet as a thought. "Work it out." Two minutes later, the pup delivered the rooster to hand.

The man kneeled and cupped the chiseled muzzle in his palms. "Not the best piece of bird work I've seen," he said, smiling and caressing the dog with soft words, "but I'll take it." In reality, it was a very decent piece of work for a young dog, and the man knew it. But he would not allow himself the luxury of seeing it as a breakthrough. The next bird, then those that followed, would tell him if this morning was a crossroads in the dog's life or a fluke—a single, complete performance that would not be repeated.

During the days ahead, he would think about the details of what had happened. He would think of his role and the springer's, of how expectation and reality can be so far apart in so many ways, of how he had hoped for everything and seen little, then expected nothing and received a gift. Mostly, he would ponder the wisdom in the old-timer's words that "... a good dog will put it together ... as often as not, when you don't expect it."

For now, though, it was enough to kneel under the building sun and tell the springer that he was the best thing since canned peaches. It was enough to look into the dog's exquisite eyes and, once again, search out a dream of perfection.

Part II

The Middle Years

Man has done no more than correct the dog's
instinctive style of hunting, molding it to the
convenience of a collaboration.
—José Ortega y Gasset

9
Looking
Backward

"Come into the shed with me," the old man said to his nine-year-old grandson. "I'll show you more pictures of my dogs." The shed was the grandfather's getaway, a small outbuilding crammed to its low rafters with hard-used hunting gear, fishing equipment, books, magazines, and mounted game. The rough plank walls were overlaid with photographs of hunting trips, of old-fashioned-looking men with dogs and birds, and of dogs alone—mainly springer spaniels and English pointers. Rising like a tall, wide throne in the shed's center was a homemade wooden recliner covered with cast-off patchwork quilts and topped with a buffalo rug.

The boy stroked the coarse buffalo hair as he sat on the recliner and stared at the photos. He listened to his grandfather speak of dogs and days that were locked in grainy black and white, and memorialized in an old man's memory. It was just the third time the boy had been in his grandfather's shed, and he was thrilled by it.

The boy, now a man, held the photograph carefully, the tips of his fingers touching only the wrinkled edges where it was glued to cardboard backing. The image was large, well-composed, and except for the wrinkling of glue—untouched by time. Its lines were sharp, its subjects clearly defined. He had looked at the enlarged photograph often, each time removing it from a storage box, then easing it from the protective envelope before dusting it with a soft cloth. It was unclear to him why he spent so much time with that particular picture, why he was drawn to it, and why it touched him as it did. He didn't know precisely what he sought in its details, though the obvious part of it was a glimpse into his own history.

He stared deeply into the photograph, as if by sheer intensity he might penetrate the black-and-white surface and mine the unknowns hidden in another dimension. By now, he knew the print intimately, yet each time he studied it, he seemed to find more of its essence. It was like a perfectly written poem that pulls at a reader and demands effort upon mental effort to extract full and true meaning.

A quick scan of this photo offered little beyond an image of a man, two dogs, and a long stringer of ducks hung on a buckboard full of gear, grub boxes, and tents. A note on the cardboard backing reminded him that the man was his grandfather, the dogs were springer spaniels named Ring and Rose, and the year was 1911. There was no mention of place. It could have been anywhere; his grandfather had cut a wide swath.

He and his grandfather were of different times and of different backgrounds. Vastly different demands had been placed on each of them and had molded them into different men. Yet, they were alike: They had the same narrow face; the same hawkish Scottish-Irish nose; the same thin lips, cleft chin, and receding hairline. They even grew similar mustaches three-quarters of a century apart. Harder lines on the grandfather's face marked a harder life, but the grandson knew that even those lines would come to him in time.

Because of distance, he had seen his grandfather perhaps seven or eight times in his life, though as family rumor had it, they were, indeed, very much alike. He had always felt relaxed and at ease around this grandfather that he barely knew, and then knew only as an old man. Later in his life, when he was mature enough to think about it,

*he came to believe that his family was right, that he and his grand-
father were close to being duplicates who had skipped a generation.*

His usual first scan finished, he moved his eyes slowly from
left to right across the photo. Dark clouds layered the sky
above the man, then faded—scattered by distance, as though a
storm had broken up. His grandfather was wearing denim
pants tucked into high, lace-up boots. The heavy-looking,
faded canvas jacket gleamed against the dark of the buckboard.
A felt slouch hat, creased in the center, was tilted back on his
grandfather's head. The young face had the same solemn, un-
smiling expression that he remembered on an old and wrinkled
countenance more than forty years later. The shotgun resting in
the crook of his grandfather's arm was a long-barreled, Winchester Model 1897 pump, a "cornshucker hammergun," as his
grandfather had called it. The old man let him handle that gun,
or another like it, just before he died.

*"This is the second-best shotgun ever made," his grandfather said
with authority as he handed the boy a gun that was nearly as long as
the youngster was tall. "Crank it open first, and make sure that it's
empty. I know I just did that, but always do it again. Look into the
chamber. That way, you know it's empty, and you'll never shoot yourself or anyone else." He let the boy fondle the big shotgun and helped
him ease it to his shoulder. Then the old man said, "I've killed a lot
of ducks and geese with that cornshucker. For that matter, I've shot a
lot of everything with it. But the best gun I've ever owned is a Winchester Model 12 pump." Even then, the boy knew enough about
guns to roughly follow what his grandfather was telling him. In a
rare moment of outright humor, the old man had smiled and added,
"Birds in a dozen states got religion when they saw my Model 12
come out of its case."*

He always saved his grandfather's dogs until last, passing quickly over the line of ducks, the big wheels of the buckboard, the shotgun scabbards lashed to its seat, and the team of roans standing hipshot with their noses buried in grain bags. Both springers looked large, weighing around fifty pounds, he guessed, though one—the male, Ring—seemed to be bigger and to have more heft. As his grandfather noted on the photo's backing, Ring was standing, looking straight at the camera, while Rose was sitting, head tilted up and to the side, staring at her owner. Although the younger man had known the importance of dogs in his grandfather's life, it was reinforced by the note. Beyond recording his name and the year, the grandfather had written only of the dogs. There was no mention of anything else—not even his hunting partners.

The note identified Ring and Rose as littermates, five years old. They came from a line that was bred out of British stock by an unnamed hunting friend. That his grandfather and cronies hunted behind imported English springers was unusual in and of itself in those days—doubly so given that it was rare for any of them to have more than a couple of silver dollars in their pockets at any time.

Because the dogs were littermates, they were almost identical in appearance. Both had broad, blocky heads; heavily-boned legs; wide chests and thick, wavy coats that were mostly dark—liver in all likelihood. Both dogs had a bit of white on their chests; thin, pencil-line blazes; and a smattering of white splotches on their rumps. He could see Ring's tail; if it had been docked at all, little had been taken off. The pair looked like what they were: hunting dogs that could do a day's work.

Each time he studied his grandfather's spaniels, he couldn't help comparing them to the springers now lying on the floor beside him. His dogs looked contemporary, like updated versions of the real thing. They were thinner and less substantial; leggier but with less bone; narrower in the head with eyes and ears closer set. White was their primary color, the contrasting liver almost an afterthought. It wasn't that his grandfather's springers were better looking; by most modern standards they were not. But they were different. His grandfather's dogs gave the impression of endurance, the ability to handle the long haul, while his own springers looked like sprinters. He knew for a fact that the spaniels sleeping beside him, even when well-conditioned, would fade after two hours of hunting, at the outside. Ring and Rose, on the other hand, looked to be all-day dogs.

"Back in the dark ages," the old man said to the boy, looking down at him with a hint of a smile in his eyes, "when I was young and hunted all the time—likely more than I should have—we didn't have trucks and kennels to carry a bunch of dogs. Those we took had to hunt long and hard with nothing more than plenty of food first and an afternoon off now and then. Whatever we needed on a trip we had to tote on horseback or buckboard, depending on the land, so we didn't have any frills. Trucks would have made it easier, but none of us had them until later on.

"We usually hunted a lot of different game—there was more around then. Almost always ducks in the morning, quail if we were far enough south, then sharptails and some pheasant, and prairie chickens in the late afternoon. We did the same thing the next day and the next, until we got tired of it and headed home. We hunted all the way back.

"On trips like that, I favored a brace of springers over other dogs. If you've got a couple of good spaniels and have them trained the right way, there's damn little that you can't hunt with them, other than bears. I never was much of a bear hunter anyway, so

that didn't bother me. In fact, here is a piece of advice for when you get around to owning your own dogs. All a reasonable man needs to hunt any bird in this country—and I've hunted most of 'em at one time or another—is two good English pointers and two good springer spaniels. Anything else is a waste of dog food.

"Next time you're here, I'll tell you about my pointers and how we hunted north for partridge and woodcock. Those were some of my favorite trips."

The grandson found it strange that after all the years that had passed he still remembered his grandfather's words, or thought he did, which amounted to the same thing. He found it even more curious that he believed them. He had owned quite a few dogs since he had been on his own—fairly decent dogs that included English setters and various retrievers. And it was possible that he would own those breeds again. But he knew his grandfather was right—that for a rough-shooting hunter, anything other than pointers and springers was "a waste of dog food."

He held the photograph loosely, still examining the image, but nearing the end of his time with it. Now, he returned to his grandfather's face, still probing for hints of the man inside, a man apparently much like himself. His grandfather had left a good many tracks over a long life, but where did they lead? Did they lead anywhere?

Who was this man staring out at him from the one-dimensional, flat paper? Who was his grandfather, really? He would never know. The connections to the past were gone; the personal ties were lost forever. Except for the intriguing but dead history of photographs, backed by rumor and childhood recollections, he could only extrapolate his links to times gone by—to dogs, bird hunts, and a grandfather passed into history.

Most of what the grandson had learned about this unusual

man was hearsay. His grandfather was a family legend of questionable judgment, a man who had fished, hunted, and followed gun dogs for the bulk of his eighty-odd years—to the exclusion of serious business and to the on-going detriment of a wife and seven children.

During a moment of self-examination triggered, perhaps, by looks backward and a spasm of guilt, his grandfather said abstractedly—more to himself than his too-young grandson—"I've never owned more than a small pot to piss in, but I've been a lot of places, had a fair number of fine dogs, and killed more birds than you'll probably see in your lifetime. I had a hell of a good time. I suppose that counts for something."

That was the last time he saw his grandfather. Six months later, the old man died quietly and without fanfare, reclining on the buffalo rug in his shed, full of years, and surrounded by a past that he hoped counted for something.

10
An Ordinary Morning

Winter fog veiled the shadowed pair snugged down into a toss of driftwood logs. Vapor hung on the dawn, worn and gauzy in close, then freshening to a thick cloak out over the water. Moisture beaded on the shoulders of the hunter's parka, on his oily gun barrel, on his Labrador's sleek-black coat. The air was cold—near the raw edge of freezing, where a few degrees would turn the nebulous mist into tangible crystals. Given the season, it appeared an ordinary morning.

The blanketed marsh thought so, too. Within the surround of predawn fog, mallards went about their business, chuckling in whispers one moment, pouring out raucous guffaws the next. The splashes of mergansers punctuated the sound of the river lapping its rock-fringed banks like a dog taking a casual drink.

Invisible wings whistled over the blind, shocking wooden thumps from the Labrador's heavy tail. He whined lightly, focused on the opaque curtain out of which the ducks would appear—suddenly and without warning—as they had done so many times. He was a veteran dog, but still anxious that life was passing him by on the wings of each fog-bound bird.

"Hush now," the hunter said, reaching over the short space between them to touch the Lab's ear. He rubbed its leathery tip with his thumb and forefinger. "Stay quiet." His voice stroked the dog as softly as his fingers. "We haven't missed a thing." The hunter looked at his dog's head; though it was obscure in the anemic half-light, he knew its broadly chiseled detail as well as he knew his own reflection. The head was solid and honest, like the brain it held and the body behind it.

Secretly, the man was pleased that the Lab had not lost his puppyish zeal and free-spirited drive for the hunt during the seven seasons they had been together. He had seen too many dogs, for too many sad reasons, without heart for the work. The Labrador at his side was not one of those dogs. Early on, the retriever had given himself to the man and to waterfowling, and when they came together the dog was at his best. And that best had become as good as the man had ever owned or, likely, would ever own, though he sometimes lost sight of it in the dog's steady, day-after-day performance.

The retriever was what he was bred to be—a working gun dog, nothing more. But, then, nothing more was necessary. He had never competed in a field trial nor run in a hunt test. He had never been in demand as a stud, nor had anyone tried to buy him. His performance was workmanlike and reliable, which made it look ordinary. It was not. He was a hunting dog, which is another way of saying that beneath the appearance of the commonplace lay the extraordinary.

The Labrador's head twisted upward as the white stillness was broken by the rush of wings. Six mallards beat low behind the jumble of driftwood, out of the marshes, pushed down by the fog and seeking the river. They passed the dark lumps that were decoys, then disappeared as though erased by the swipe of a hand. Soft, coercing calls from the hunter tensed the Lab, sent a tremor down his body, and riveted his eyes ahead into the thin hint of breeze. Another set of chuckles and the ducks were there, conjured by the calls, backpedaling, their feet down above the blocks.

The dog's eyes locked on the tumbled drake before it arced to the water, lost in the fog. He stayed on his mark, wide-eyed and rigid, until the hunter spoke his name and said, "Dead." At these words, an excitement-driven "Yip" launched the dog from the driftwood. Five running leaps and he was in the river, an inky line rulered from the blind to the spot where he had last seen the drake. Then he, too, was absorbed by the fog.

"Good boy," the man said, when the Lab had placed the mallard in his hand. "Good job." He fussed over the dog, telling him as he had so often, that the Lab was the best fellow that ever wore a collar. And the hunter meant it.

The man had long ago come to grips with the little "Yip" that fired a retrieve, and he accepted the dog's tendency on his returns to make for the nearest bank and finish the retrieve on land. Both had become irrelevant. The Lab's marks and lines to downed birds were arrow true; if he chose to escape the icy water on the way back that was his affair. The man was his only judge, and he considered it sensible. The dog never dropped a bird, never paused in his delivery. Only when he had placed a retrieved duck in his hunter's hand would he relax, shake, and nose the game he had given up—and given up willingly, without a hint of reluctance.

This astounded the man. Although he had trained the lab, watched him develop, and made the retriever part of his life—along with quite a few other dogs—he was still amazed by the animal's willingness to go against embedded drives. This dog was steady to shot and to fall, took signals well, and delivered to hand—when the mindless instincts of millennia told him bark and chase, run like hell after the bird, grab it, and eat it on the spot. That he did none of those things, the man thought, was what made each retrieve a singular and truly incredible event.

The man understood the behavioral theories and hands-on

mechanics of training; nevertheless, he remained enchanted by quality dog work with its ritualized choreography of grace and beauty. But in his mind, the difficulty or style of the retrieves was not the most remarkable factor in that piece of the hunting equation called a gun dog. Even at the lowest level of skill, he knew that there was something far from ordinary underlying each cooperative performance. The wonder of retrievers was not in superficial judgments of how well they performed; it was hidden within the dogs, in the depths of what they did willingly, and why they did it at all.

Full dawn, such as it was, kicked in on schedule, and the mist, like a collection of tired night spirits, began to fade beneath the gaining light. Cottony wisps of fog disappeared from above the toss of driftwood logs and unraveled over the river. Shapes hardened and acquired texture. The dark lumps on the water became bobbing decoys and shadows etched themselves into the hunter and his dog snugged down on a riverbank. For a time, the air would chill, then slowly yield its grip to a pale sun.

Given the season, it appeared to be an ordinary morning.

11

Terms
of Devotion

We met in a ruffed grouse covert during the heart of October, strangers wandering the same shining woodland. I was sitting, then, on a granite cornerstone that anchored the tumbled lengths of two old walls and linked their purposes at a common point—an end or a beginning, depending on how one saw it. A stunning cock grouse and two woodcock lay next to me, cooling in the morning air.

Few people knew of this place, which was tucked and hidden inside an expanse of timber, well away from any traveled road. In the proprietary way of bird hunters, I thought of the covert as mine, and I was put off by the presence of a man walking a trampled-wide deer trail edging one of the walls. My dog announced him with a breathy "Woof," then in spaniel fashion beat the air with his tail.

"Good morning," he said, in a pleasant though very formal and oddly disconnected voice, looking more at my springer than at me. "I hope that I'm not interfering." He looked around the woods and added, "I had forgotten how beautiful this spot and these walls are in the fall. I haven't been here in several years." Indeed, it was splendid with the sun streaming grandly through rich aspens and maples, dappling fallen leaves and the ageless gray of stones, glinting off clusters of a light frost that clung futilely beneath low pines.

The man was lean and looked fit; I judged him to be in his early forties. His clothes were clean and unwrinkled, but worn soft and stained with time. He broke his shotgun, a high-grade Parker 20-gauge with a patina of both wear and care on its surface, and set the gun gently on the wall. He did not have a dog.

"That's an elegant grouse," he said, gesturing with a slight shift of his chin. "Look at the tail and ruff; they're perfect." Then he asked, "Did your dog work the bird?" He smiled, looking again at the springer.

"Good," he said, nodding his head after I told him that, as a rule, I don't shoot birds the dog doesn't flush. "That's good," he repeated. "Though some think it silly or elitist, it's neither. It's the right thing to do." As if reading my mind about the contradiction of what he had said and hunting without a dog, he mentioned that he had flushed three grouse but didn't shoot much any more.

He reached into a side pocket of his vest and pulled out a small dog biscuit. A whistle hanging from a dark, braided lanyard slid out with the treat. The man stared at the plastic and oiled leather for a long moment. "I'm still foolish enough to carry these things around after all this time." I had the distinct impression that he was speaking to my dog, not to me.

"Would you mind if I give him this biscuit?" he asked, when he had folded the whistle and lanyard back into the pocket. I didn't mind and told the man I appreciated his asking. He knelt and held the treat where the dog could take it easily and not have to snap for it. "Good boy. You're a fine fellow." He spoke softly, then began a light and rhythmic scratching of the dog's ears. The fingers of one hand moved in quick appraisal to the spaniel's neck, over his chest, and down his leg.

"I like your dog—how he's put together and the straightforward way he looks you in the eye," the man said in a manner that told me not only did he mean it, but he knew something about gun dogs.

"I've always fancied setters, myself," he continued, "and I've been lucky enough to have had some nice ones, but it's hard to top a good field springer. I've had wonderful hunts with them. Besides, they're loyal friends—with no terms to their devotion—and that's a great thing."

An airy breeze scurried along the earth before lifting skyward to swirl and play through the trees. Leaves began whispering, one to another, like mischievous children. The spaniel rolled his eyes at the sounds, then relaxed and rested his chin on the man's knee. Maybe it was that small gesture of acceptance that triggered the rush of words.

"I've owned or been around bird dogs all of my life," he said, suddenly, as though he had made an instant decision to speak. "At least, until three years ago," he added, still looking down at my springer. "Nearly thirty years back, my father started breeding his own line of English setters"—he named the line—"and I went in with him part time when I finished college. But we didn't do it for money. My family was comfortable, so money was neither an objective nor an issue."

"We bred and trained our setters for the love of doing it, as our own gun dogs, for friends, and—occasionally—for a few other special people. We never had more than a litter every two or three years, sometimes even four years, and I'm not being arrogant when I say that the pups were worth the wait." I thought I had heard of the dogs and started to ask for details, but his story kept moving, running through time until he hit the point.

"At the end, I had three setters that were my personal dogs." He had his open palm on my springer's head, barely touching it, as if reassuring himself that the dog was there.

"You know how it happens. With a dozen wonderful dogs around, there's no explaining why a couple of them capture your heart and hold on to it forever." I understood and nodded to let him know.

"I'm ashamed to say this," he went on, "but I loved those three dogs as much as I loved my family. Two of them were six-year-old males, littermates that I always ran as a brace. The youngest was only two and already magical. She was a dog of dreams, the kind that brought tears to my eyes. Everything— and I don't say that casually—everything that I wanted was born into her."

The man stopped abruptly, then pushed out the rest in a voice thin with barely suppressed vehemence. "All three of those dogs died in the same bird season. They were killed in separate accidents—trivial, freakish accidents, the sort of things that wouldn't happen again in ten lifetimes. I almost quit hunting after my males died. When I lost the youngster, I buried her on our property with the others, turned the kennels back to my father, and walked away. I never went near the dogs again. Or picked up a shotgun. Until today.

"I don't know why," he admitted, "but this morning, I needed to walk familiar ground, see a grouse, look at the leaves and these old walls, and carry my favorite bird gun. Maybe I just wanted to see autumn again, to make sure it still existed as I remembered it. Whatever the reason, I'm glad I came out. It's been a long time."

There was nothing I could say. I had lost much-loved dogs, but my degree of loss was nothing compared to what I had just heard. I did the obvious and asked him to hunt out the morning with my dog and me.

"No, no thanks," he answered, as he reached to the wall and lifted his Parker. "I really appreciate the offer." He leaned over, cupped my dog's chin in his hand and looked into his eyes.

"I would love to watch this fellow work, but I had better get home. I have to resolve a bit of unfinished business; something important that I've been putting off for too long."

About fifty yards up the deer trail, the man stopped and turned to look back at us. He smiled and raised his hand, then walked away. Once again, I was left with the near-certainty that he had smiled and waved at my springer.

12
The $41,000 Dog

"I am thinking seriously about buying my own dog," my good friend and long-time hunting partner said to me out of the corner of his mouth. Jim's elbows were propped on the bar, supporting his head, apparently to steady his vision as he plumbed the deep-amber depths of his mug of beer. "In fact, I've got the basics—like breed—pretty well thought out, but I need your opinion on some details.

"Don't take this the wrong way," he continued, pulling his eyes away from the mug and turning toward me, "but I'm getting tired of always hunting behind your springers. They do a nice job and all that, but I've never owned a dog. I think its time that I got my own. Know what I mean?"

I assured Jim that I knew exactly what he meant, then reminded him that I had been talking up his owning a gun dog for some years.

"I know you have," he admitted, "and now I'm going to do something about it. But I'm going with an English pointer. Flushing dogs, like yours, don't do much for me."

Jim started obliterating a wet spot on the bar, rubbing it mindlessly with his forefinger, making a rhythmic, aggravating squeak before he outlined his thoughts—such as they were.

Once he had the spot dry and, thankfully, squeakless, he said, "I plan to get a finished dog, a mature dog, with all of its training in place. I don't have the time or know-how to work a pup or even a well-started youngster. And I'm not afraid of putting some bucks into a good dog. So, how about laying out for me your best guess of the price tag?"

I told him that he was looking at at least $4,000, and more likely as high as $6,000 or $7,000, for a well-bred, professionally finished English pointer from a big-name trainer.

"I can do that," Jim pushed in quickly. "Actually, I thought I'd have a bit more than that in up-front cost."

I assured him that he would, indeed, have "a bit more than that in up-front cost." I reminded him that because he had hunted with me for so many years, he had absolutely no equipment beyond his hunting clothes and a shotgun—no dog gear at all, not even a basic lead. He would have to buy everything.

"How bad could it be?" Jim asked, raising his eyebrows, with the merest hint of a question mark in his tone. "All we're talking about is some simple stuff, like a collar and a box of biscuits. Right?"

Then he said, "Grab that napkin and make up a list, including the dog, of what I'll need to get started. Better yet, break it down into itemized costs—and a total—for the first year." If he was nothing else, Jim was a banker, methodical about money.

He called the bartender and asked for a pen, then ordered another round. I got the feeling that the new-dog idea wasn't developing to his taste.

When my list reached the bottom of the napkin, Jim leaned over for a glance at it, then lurched back on his stool and took a deep, half-choking swallow of beer.

"What the hell are you doing?" he asked in a low, beer-strangled voice. "My divorce didn't cost me that much. Well, that's not true, but you're already up in five figures—over

$11,000, if I read that right — and we're talking about a dog here." Jim grabbed the napkin for a closer look.

"Travel crates, outdoor kennel—oh, my God—necessary equipment, vet bills"—at health care, he let out another long groan—"and food. Dog food?" Customers turned and stared at him when he yelled, "Over a year, I don't spend that much on my own meals."

Jim moved rapidly down the list, eyes following finger through each item. When he reached $1,800 for three months of tune-up with the pro trainer, his face turned red as revenge, his entire body tightened, and he stress-farted violently—once again attracting customer attention. Given the pressure of the moment, it was a forgivable social error.

"Why do I have to take the dog back to the trainer?" he asked, in a near-whimper. "If I follow my schedule, I'll have had him just six or seven months! Where's the need if he's already trained?"

I explained to Jim that because I knew him so well, I was confident a few months was more than enough time for him to completely screw up even a nicely finished pointer. I knew, for a fact, that if he hoped to hunt the dog with any success during the next bird season, it would have to return to the trainer for a major overhaul. And it would have to return every year.

Jim's elbows were back on the bar, his head was back in his hands, and his eyes were again looking for answers in the now very empty beer mug.

There was one more thing that he needed, I told him. Something that he could not do without.

"Go ahead," he muttered, "one more piece of gear can't make much of a difference."

Don't be too sure about that, I said, then wrote in particularly large letters, Sport Utility Vehicle—$30,000. Jim had forgotten that the only vehicle he owned was a snazzy, two-seater, a ground-hugging sports car that couldn't make it over a curb, let alone cut it in the field or serve as transport for a high-powered pointer.

At least a minute passed before Jim let go of his head, dropped his arms to the bar, turned to me, and—with considerable gravity in his voice—said, "You know, the more I think about it, the more I realize just how much I've enjoyed hunting with you and your flutters for all of these seasons. How long has it been? Must be at least fifteen years."

Then he wadded up the cost-list napkin; flashed a wide, toothy smile; and put his arm around my shoulder before going on. "It seems criminal to break up a fine bird-hunting relationship because I was selfish enough to want my own dog. I was being small-minded, even childish; I understand that now. No matter how much it hurts me to do it, in the interest of our long partnership, I'm going to put my personal needs on the back burner. I'll think about a dog some other time.

"What do you say we have another round," he said, smile intact, "and talk about something else."

13
Doin' Nothin'

Winter lingers, shoving doggedly at the storm windows, rattling panes already loosened by other winters. A solitary leaf, a dull-crimson survivor that has persisted for five months on a maple just outside my office window, gives up and allows the wind to gust it away and take it where it will.

I have watched that lone leaf daily; I have seen it drooping and sodden in rain, thrashed and beaten by storms, plastered with heavy snow. And now, nearing the end of a hard season, it takes off, apparently tired of hanging around in bad weather.

Like me. Like my dogs, though they are better than I am at doin' nothin'.

I am sitting on the warm side of the storm windows, listening to their irritating tap-and-rattle, watching winter's strength gradually diminish under the power of the approaching spring equinox. Piles of dark, nasty clouds scud from the north to blot out the sky and throw down feeble spatterings of sleet. Wind lunges at the now leafless maple with brief and harmless bursts of energy. Winter is an old and weakened fighter, yet it seems reluctant to yield the seasonal match to its youthful opponent.

All things considered, it is a lousy day.

Small yips, like distant bird calls, rise from an aging spaniel sprawled on my office floor. These cries harmonize with the rhythmic scratching of paws on wood—dog dreams. Perhaps of October days light and airy as a wish; of coverts and fields extravagant with earth smells; of woodcock, grouse, pheasants. It is just as likely, though, that the yipping twitches are visions of endless bowls of dog chow. Or the non-dreams of boredom.

My other spaniel, younger and awake with restless vitality—maybe due to a youthful shortage of dream material—looks at me, his springer eyes brown and attentive and questioning, but out of context within confining office walls. There is powerful life radiating from those eyes, but for now he lays his head back on his paws and follows the lead of his top-dog uncle, who is resigned to doing nothing.

Dogs have a wonderful capacity to do nothing, to just rest and doze, stare blankly out of half-opened lids, stretch and yawn, then ball up to rest again. And they come by it naturally. Their wild-dog brethren—wolves and coyotes—rest through the bulk of each day, rousing themselves to action only with good cause. I admire many things about the family of dogs, most everything, in fact. But I especially admire their ability to relax completely, to kill time, to disconnect and marshal their energy when there is nothing to do but wait. Maybe envy is a better word than admire, because I relax so badly.

Like now, when a time set aside for leisure is being threatened by guilt emanating from stacks of neglected paperwork.

"To hell with work," I tell the dogs, "Let's go."

They are up in an instant, watching me, sleep forgotten. Then they are out of the office and waiting—up on their toes and dancing in place, tails moving air—down where the good stuff is stored: the coats and boots and guns, the orange collars, the leads, the retrieving dummies. Dog things. But we are bringing none of them. We are just leaving, taking off like the windblown maple leaf, getting in the truck and driving away on my arguable theory that it is more fun doin' nothin' outside, surrounded by lousy weather, than breaking a brain inside, surrounded by lousy windows.

To my springers, doing something is the undeniable reality of moving, the reason for the energy-storing rest and the doldrums of tolerant waiting. Once again, their approach to life, their innate patience and acceptance of circumstance, have proven correct. If they do nothing long enough, something is bound to happen. With such a broad-based philosophy, they can't go wrong. Particularly with me, who lacks their skills at marking time and whose winter-bludgeoned mind needs frequent repair.

We are on a weak ridge now, three fugitives from tedium who have gone over the mountain just to see what we can see. And that hasn't been much. But no matter. Quality comes in many forms, and today theirs is simply getting out. Mine is watching them quarter barren hillsides and hunt gray swales through the season's confusion of green sproutings and the hint of new buds, through its dead leaves and brown mud offset with sugary patches of snow.

My younger dog, the keener of the pair, works a too-early woodcock, pushes it airborne, and drops cleanly at the flush. I thank him for the fine job on a day when nothing was expected. We walk through an autumn of the mind and, though sleet-pelted and wind-chilled, we are all breathing new air.

Below us, down from the ridge, a sizable alder run shows through the spindly shanks of an old apple orchard mixed with invading pines. The covert is a favored October haunt, a place of moist earth and sun-speckled quiet, of grouse and woodcock—a place made for hunters and their dogs. I cannot understand all of its workings, but because I am so involved with the covert I have tried to know it intimately, personally, as I have tried to know the springers at my side.

We will not go into the covert today. The unexpected woodcock took refuge in its alders and will find living tough enough without the intrusive pressure of another flush. Besides, we are not out in the late-winter funk to chase birds, train, or pseudo-hunt; we are supposed to be out here doin' nothin'.

So we sit. And look. I with collar high and hat low, the dogs snugged against my legs with wind fingering their wet fur. For a brief moment, the heavy rolls of clouds collapse, and columns of brightness stroke the skinny apple trees and warm the cold green of the pines.

Seasons of memories run with the light. Sharp vignettes of dogs and birds and friends race from the past through my mind's eye. Some of the scenes are disjointed and overlapped, like the out-of-sync frames of a badly edited movie. Others are clearly separated by time and place. Still others are single images that fade with the ephemeral columns of sun.

My springers, too, stare into the covert, but with a focused intensity unique to gun dogs. I take pleasure in thinking that, perhaps, they are conjuring memories of themselves, weaving as smooth as silken strands over the orchard floor and into the alders. Perhaps, they see themselves from afar, alive under a sun that is high and strong and dancing on dew-sparkled leaves like golden notes of music. Perhaps, they are revisiting lavish smells and hard flushes and workmanlike retrieves. Perhaps, they are wisely replenishing themselves for the next round of doin' nothin', when they will wait and sleep-hunt coverts from my office floor with only yips and twitches to signal their work.

Until the wind again rattles loose storm windows and another maple leaf, tired of hanging around, blows away. Until I, too, need to let the wind take me where it will.

14
Pilgrims

During the three seasons we hunted together, I learned almost nothing about Dirt Man—not even his name. He didn't offer it, and I didn't ask. But his pointer was called Slim. And they were an oddball twosome, a brace of grungy pilgrims slouching along their own path to some distant promised land. Both of them looked like a long streak of bad luck.

I met them on an old and purposeless track leading into the western high country, under a sun that was pounding hard for a mid-October morning. Heat wrapped the mountains in a thick skin and pulsed visibly from the earth where my setter and I were catching our breath after the climb to grouse country. Few people chased mountain grouse—ruffs or blues—in those days, so running into bird hunters was a happening—a unique happening when the hunters were Dirt Man and Slim.

My dog saw the movement first. She twisted her head and stared at a pointer that had blown around a bend in the track at full run, then pivoted, and minced—as though his feet hurt—a few steps into an edge of scrub pine. When the dog froze and leaned into the point, I knew he had cut off a running grouse and had pinned the bird neatly in front of him.

The dog was bad-looking: dingy white and mottled with

smudges of liver, thin-chested and rib-sprung, with a big, boxy head framed by little ears. Although he was as lean as a fleeting thought, knotted ropes of muscles bunched under his skin. Even with his steadiness to a close flush and shot, then with his launch at the command "Fetch," I wrote him off as an ugly pointer who had gotten lucky. Especially when he ambled out of the timber heeled to the apparition my first thought tagged as Dirt Man.

Everything about the man was the color of old earth. A nasty fedora drooped on his head like a half-dried cow pie, shading muddy crevasses around his eyes. Tangles of hair sprouted from under his hat, twining with a beard that graded seamlessly into his shirt. Of dubious origin, this garment, in turn, bagged out of pants fertile with topsoil, their cuffs riding high over boots that appeared to be clods of earth. Only his dark and weathered hands offered relief from the dull brown sameness. Dirt Man looked to be an ageless Rocky Mountain Phoenix who had risen from his own ashes—and had forgotten to dust himself off.

He was very tall—six-and-a-half feet, at least—and thin as a whippy switch. He walked down the track toward me in a loose-jointed, shambling style that suggested collapse at every step. Same with the pointer, who seemed to have burned himself out on one grouse. He shuffled along, matching the man's pace in a head-down gait that screamed exhaustion. Then I noticed that the dog wasn't even panting and that Dirt Man didn't have a drop of sweat on him. Their endurance turned out to be as deceptive as their appearance.

The man nodded, folded himself onto a nearby rock, and pulled out an apple and a honed-thin pocketknife. He shared slices with the pointer, who sat with his eyes fixed on the man, not the food. It was clear that the dog adored Dirt Man, who pushed back his cow-pie hat, looked at the sweat running down my forehead, and in a rich baritone said, "Warm, today." Dirt Man was not much of a talker.

I never found out where he came from, but his accent hinted at the northern Midwest, and twice he mentioned woodcock, asking if I had ever hunted them. "Fine bird, woodcock," he said. "Too slow for gunslingers, but for a man and a dog, they're the best. Woodcock are the thing I miss living out here." Looking down at his pointer he added, "I'd like to try Slim on woodcock. He's pretty good on most birds."

After a season loosely partnered with Dirt Man, I realized that calling Slim "pretty good" was on par with summing up the Rockies as "nice hills." Under the pointer's mud-ugly surface was the finest working gun dog I had ever shot over. Ruffed and blue grouse, chukars, pheasants, and the quail we found along rivers—Slim worked them all perfectly. He had a big nose, experience, and magical bird sense. He was steady to wing and shot, but would flush on command, then resteady. And he was an immaculate retriever. Slim had all of the right stuff. And, for his chosen way of life, so did Dirt Man.

By any broad societal measure, Dirt Man was quite a few notes out of tune. Most people, then, would have called him a "survivalist" or a "back-to-earth" type or a "hippie," or whatever the current term was for someone who didn't flow with the mainstream. But they would have been wrong; Dirt Man had no social agenda. He had simply chosen to "live away," as he phrased it, alone and tucked into the mountains, unwashed and uncurried, training his pointers, and hunting birds. Once, I asked him why, being a loner, he stopped and talked with me the first time.

"You had a bird dog," he said. "Most I see up here don't. They're deer and elk hunters," he added flatly, without judgment or disdain. Dirt Man was just a pilgrim listening to his own rhythms and allowing other people to do the same.

As well as being a first-class woodsman and wing shot, Dirt Man was an intuitive gun-dog trainer. He was bringing up two pups out of Slim, homely lookalikes and both—at eighteen-months—showing the same savvy and skills. He seemed to look into dogs' heads, judge what was there, then make them think that what he wanted from them was exactly what they wanted to do. Dirt Man was calm, fair, and—as far as I knew—totally lacking in harshness. Dogs loved being around him. Dirt Man met three of my dogs and, each time, they seemed unable to stay away from him.

"If bird dogs don't trust you," he told me in a rare moment of chattiness, as he rubbed the back of one of my Labradors, "you might as well not have them. Any fool can train a good dog to hunt, but without trust you've lost whatever it is that makes them want to hunt as a team. Not just for you, but with you. When a bird dog works with you, then you've got yourself a real hunter."

Dogs, in fact all animals, trusted Dirt Man. They were drawn to him. The last time we met, he showed up with a coyote pup gamboling around his legs and nipping Slim's feet. "I've about got this little guy to flash point," he said, glancing at me with a hint of a smile. "But he'll be tough to steady." Dirt Man might have managed it.

Dirt Man, Slim, and his pups—the whole menagerie—disappeared near the end of the third season I knew them. He didn't announce his departure, and I didn't know where he camped, so there were no good-byes. I knew he was gone only because he failed to show up at any of our meeting points. In keeping with his style, he left quietly without fuss or fanfare.

Perhaps, like all sojourners who are more than they seem at first glance, he was touched by a sudden urge to wander

and took off one clear, mountain morning in search of a
new shrine. I hope so. Without true pilgrims like Dirt Man
slouching toward it, there can be no promised land.

15
Changing Needs

The blind was wrapped in dark, thick quiet broken only by the awakenings of distant geese. Close in, there were more immediate sounds—the rustlings of clothes and shufflings of ponderous boots, the dull thunk of a dropped shotgun shell, breathy snuffs from a young Labrador testing the morning breeze.

Within the pit, the two men were nothing to each other but bulky shapes, sensed more than seen across the few feet that separated them. They were strangers thrown together by chance for a few hours. They had said good morning at breakfast, eaten quietly, and spoken little during the ride to the field. One was right-handed, while the other was a lefty, so spotting themselves in the blind needed few words.

By nature, neither man was outgoing or talkative, especially with strangers. If it hadn't been for the Labrador sitting outside, at the blind's edge, each man would have been content to shoot geese and keep talk to a minimum. It surprised them both when they struck up a conversation.

A wooden kitchen match burned away the darkness for an instant, then paused in front of a middle-aged, weather-creased face. "Do you mind if I smoke?" a gravelly voice asked around a pipe stem. "I won't if it bothers you."

"Doesn't bother me at all," The voice was rapid-fire,

younger sounding, and disembodied in the murky pit. "I quit a couple of months ago and still crave the smell." A second match flared and died to a glow, then the rich fragrance of tobacco drifted over the blind. A pair of violent sneezes erupted from the Labrador, followed by watery, nose-clearing snorts. His owner chuckled. "Seems Jack doesn't appreciate good Burley. Don't worry about it."

"Sometimes I forget how rough tobacco must be on a dog's nose," the smoker said, shelving his pipe next to an open box of shells. "I'll wait 'til the wind kicks up a touch." His head gesture toward the Lab went unseen in a predawn that was just hinting at daylight, but his words were sharply defined.

"I've always liked the name Jack for a dog. It's simple, to the point, and not foolish. I've used it twice over the years, and one of those Jacks was the best Labrador I've ever owned." He hesitated, as if he was tossing something around in his mind, then added abruptly, "Or ever will own."

The building clamor of geese had Jack up on his toes, his neck stretched, as he tried to sort out the raucous noise flowing in from all directions. The dog's head whipped sharply upward at the wing whistles of a flock of ducks beating over the decoys. He whined lightly, twice, before his owner put a hand on his back and said, "Quiet," then "Down." Both commands were barely above a whisper. The Lab dropped instantly onto a pile of camouflage netting alongside the pit. Other than brief scratchings as he settled in, he did not move or make another sound.

"He's a youngster, not quite two," the man said apologetically. "He's hard-headed and has a lot to learn, but Jack is going to be a good one." He flipped up his collar and tucked the tandem of lanyard-hung whistles into his parka. "In fact, I haven't decided if he is too good a field-trial prospect to hunt, or too good a gun dog not to hunt. That's why I brought him this morning."

The wind was shifting, easing around at an angle behind them and blowing away from the dog. There was the sparking snap of a match, and pipe smoke lofted on the freshening breeze. It rose into a sky smudged by contrasting fingers of gray and blotched with dingy wet clouds, a sky now light enough to show a sprawl of land as bleak as a front porch to nowhere. Wavering strings of ducks and stiff lines of geese were stacked high on the faint streak of horizon.

The older man drew softly on his pipe, looked past his hunting partner, and stared hard at the Labrador, still half-hidden in the gloom. His eyes ran knowingly over the dog, from the profile of its squared-up head, down the muscled shoulders and rump, to the slightly wagging tip of thick tail. He said, "Even lying down, Jack's a fine looking Labrador. As nicely built as I've seen in some years."

At his name, the dog turned his head, thumped his tail, then went back to sky watching. "Sounds like you know Labradors," Jack's owner said.

"I've had Labs for more than twenty-five years," the other hunter answered, nodding his head. "And nothing but them for most of that time." The man scratched his cheek, his fingers rasping against morning stubble. "I raised and trained my own line for a while—a small operation, just a litter every year or so. I trialed some of my top dogs."

His voice paused, then lowered, as though he had surprised himself with his words. "Actually, I was into the whole trial game seriously for about fifteen years."

"Do you mind telling me your name?" the younger man asked.

At the answer he said, "I've heard about you and your Labradors. The word around the circuit is that they were first-class dogs." There was a touch more respect in his tone when he asked, "Did you quit trialing for any particular reason?" Then he caught himself and added, "That may not be any of my affair."

"Let's just say that I got tired of nearly everything that went with hard training and stiff competition. It wasn't the dogs; I still love the breed, maybe more than ever. But now I have them—just a couple—for what they are, not for what they can do." He hesitated, looked again at the alert Labrador, then seemed to come to a decision.

"I've not talked about this with many people," the man said in a subdued voice. "I suppose the reason I'm telling you is that you're a stranger I'll never see again, and if you run the national trial circuit you've likely heard the story anyway.

"That Jack dog I mentioned," he continued, "the best I've ever owned? I ruined him—killed him in the end, if I'm being truthful—trying to win it all at a big trial. It was heat stroke. I pushed him too hard, too long, on too hot a day. When I carried him off the field, I swore that I'd never do that, or anything like that, to another dog. He spent two weeks in a clinic and came out of it with heart and brain damage. He lived less than a year. During that time, he could barely walk from the kennel to the house. Then he didn't know where he was when he got there."

The man went on, hurriedly, talking more to himself than the stranger across the blind. "After Jack died, I found homes for my Labs and tore down my whole kennel. I kept two of the softest tempered, least talented dogs and brought them into the house to live with me. I expect nothing from them other than happy companionship and picking up a bird now and again when we hunt alone. It may seem strange to you, at your point in life, but I've never been as content or enjoyed dogs more than I do these days."

"You're right," the other man broke into the wordless lull that followed, "I have heard the story. And I'm sorry about your dog, but things like that happen. It's no reason to quit what you love." He pointed at his dog, fully focused on the birds starting to fill the sky, and spoke emphatically, "If I lost this dog today, as much as I care about him, I'd be running another one tomorrow."

"I saw it that way too, years ago, but not any more," the older man said, between puffs on his dark-stained pipe. "Things don't just happen; we make them happen, or, worse, let them happen. And, in all honesty, I'm not sure how much I loved the training and trialing. At first, maybe, until competition became an obsession, and I blurred the line between what I was winning and what I was losing. When my dogs became nothing more than living means to a dead end, there was a kennel full of reasons to quit.

"Don't get me wrong," he followed up quickly, in an effort to smooth over any tension he might have created. "I love to watch well-handled, high-powered dogs—especially up-and-coming youngsters like your Jack. I just don't own or train them any more."

He turned away and scanned the gray sky, now dropping soft snow, as if the heavy clouds were crumbling into lighter pieces. "Perfect weather," he said, smiling widely at the younger man. He picked up his shotgun and shoved shells into it, then said, "I can't wait to see Jack in action, but he won't get any work unless I stop talking. Look out there. Low, at about nine o'clock. We've got geese coming in."

16
Homestead Ghost

The granite doorstone should have read 1897. Although the eight was a casualty of boot wear and weather erosion, given the two possible dates with '97 in them, it had to be the more recent. The farmhouse could not have survived the weight of two hundred winters. But 1897 was old enough, a rarity among homesteads. And the revealing spring sun above me laid bare the crush of each year.

As had happened before, under the light of different seasons, I was standing in the present glimpsing the past. The spaniel at my side sat staring around the old place, as I was. Perhaps he, too, felt a kinship with this familiar homestead, though more likely he was winding grouse and woodcock anchored in the coverts of its land. Soon, we would seek those birds to hone the springer's off-season edges.

The dog and I had found this chunk of history on an October morning years earlier. We were hunting up a swell of ground that rose from the floor of a small valley when I broke out onto a hint of road lifting to the knoll's top. The weeded, double ruts were flanked by gnarled but living apple trees interspersed with the deadwood frames of elms. The springer was making game beneath the trees and weaving into twists of autumn-purple berry brambles that hugged the road where I had stopped.

A woodcock flushed from the thorny tangle, towered over my head, and fell to the shot within feet of me. At the sound, two grouse wing-thundered from the apple trees, one beating hard up the roadway, the other gliding down it. I took the easy one, then picked up the woodcock and called the springer, still hupped in the berries. He delivered the glider, and we moved after the up-road bird.

At the crown of the hill, where the grouse had dropped out of sight, the ruts angled left and ended in an overgrown but still visible turnaround that was once the dooryard of a house. I heeled the dog and looked off the knoll, searching for bearings that would tell me where the springer and I and the house were located. I wasn't sure of our spot in space. The morning's hunt had been a wandering, no-destination sort: I followed the dog to the birds and the birds where they took us. The springer's nose and a ruffed grouse had brought us here, to a forgotten farmhouse out of the past.

It was a study in gray, the different hues and tones depending on the part of the house and the weather to which it had been subjected. The front was silvery, bleached to a metallic shine like the barrels of a long-used shotgun. In contrast, the back was dark and moss-covered, secretive, and caved in on itself as though shamed by the decay of a century's winds and winters. Shades of plain gray dappled the sides of the house, neutral links joining the brightness of the front with the gloom of the collapsing rear. A lone cedar shake swayed from a roof beam like a tired leaf that had hung on through the winter and was ready to let go in a fresh spring breeze.

Dark window sockets stared unseeing at the brushy, grown-up dooryard. I stood in front of them, almost blinded by sharp reflections of sun angling off age-burnished wood. The house had been used hard by the decades, but the fact that the structure was still upright was mute testimony that its builder had given it staying power. This was not one of the legions of hardscrabble farmhouses that fell into their cellars a few years after their owners threw down their rock-dulled shovels and walked away from a rugged life.

It is said that an empty house is an open book on the people who lived in it. True, in some cases, though too many pages of this story were missing or faded, allowing no more than a glimpse backward here and there. But the homestead held a sense of invitation. Near the front and to one side of the house I always felt passing hints that I was not alone. It was like sensing the presence of a hunting partner who, after drifting off, walks up behind me unseen and unheard. In truth, the sensation might not have been even that dramatic. Perhaps it was more like a light breeze that, on an absolutely still day, drifts out of nowhere bearing a warm feel and welcoming fragrance.

My dog, too, sensed something beyond the norm at this homestead. There were moments when he would stop, cock his head, and listen, stare at the front of the house and around its corners. Then he would sit, his tail wagging, as though he was waiting to greet a visitor. Or waiting for his own form of epiphany, as I waited for mine. I can't speak for the dog, but I saw no apparitions. Not even in the family's sad, neglected graveyard.

This small cemetery, with its epitaphs graven in stone amid run-amok tiger lilies, recorded that the homestead's family had lost three children and one adult: a daughter and grandmother in 1911, victims of that year's flu pandemic; one son in 1917, killed in action during World War I; another son in 1921. His age-tilted stone did not say whether he was killed by a bull, tetanus, tuberculosis, or his own hand. Like the house that once sheltered its occupants, the graveyard was a history of loss. I had to look elsewhere for gains.

Property-line corners were signaled by pyramids of stones. Walls fed from these cairns, defining paths, roads, orchards, gardens, and fields that had aged into mere suggestions of what they had been. The land was a rocky network of tumble-down stone walls, where grouse tucked in on rainy days and wing-tipped birds sought refuge from my dog. Indeed, it was the rendering of the homestead's walls that offered an outline of the whole and guided me into its parts, into a few of its secrets, and into its legacy of effort.

The people of this house were apple lovers, with eyes for form and function. Five types of apple trees were clustered on the farm, and—like the stone walls—they were placed to outline facets of it. They told of paths, now invisible; fields, now grown heavy in pines; and sun-drenched slopes, now thick with aspen, graduating down to spring-watered alder runs. There were apple plantings bent and struggling with age, strings of suckered clones, and loners that had seeded themselves, perhaps via droppings from generations of grouse.

Near the gloomy rear of the house, three apple trees stood as ancient sentinels. It was to this threesome that my springer would head when I cut him loose. And it was more than ritual. He would work around and under the trees, tail windmilling, nose down, each motion screaming birds. Then he would drive in hard for the flush, always at the same spot. Never did a grouse or woodcock take to the air.

This was an experienced dog, a good trailer who rarely lost scooting grouse, wasn't fooled by old or lingering scent, and usually produced birds when he said they were near. But not from the sentinels. After a half-dozen episodes, I began calling whatever triggered him to make game "the ghost bird."

Every old place needs a ghost. And never more than on a sparkling spring morning, when the conjuring of spirits is difficult. To be sure, I wanted this homestead, with its crumbling farmhouse and chiseled doorstone, to have its ghosts. That they appeared as the lingering sense of a strong family, along with the persistent shade of a grouse or woodcock, made the thought of them doubly pleasing.

I knew without doubt that if I looked long and hard, the people and the ghost bird would create themselves in my mind's eye. But an overactive imagination would, I knew, lessen the mystery. As before, on other days, it was enough to feel a friendly breeze brush my shoulder and pause there for a moment, as if it were saying, "Take your time and look around." It was enough to watch a good gun dog search for a vague piece of the homestead's past, then give up an impossible quest and ease down the aspen slope back to the present.

17
Frozen Dawn

The creek was dark against its surround of white. It ran and twisted between snow-covered banks like a gun metal-hued ribbon crushed by a giant hand and tossed down the long length of the valley. A cloud of mist, a creation of moisture lifting into frigid air, hung over sections of the creek's surface and banks. The mist rose fifteen feet before it paused, froze, and fell, returning to its origin as artfully beautiful crystals.

The creek began as a sprawl of hot springs in the high foothills edging one side of the valley. It flowed from the benches—at times following land contours, at other points carving its own meanders in a rush to join the main river that watered the valley's lower end. From its heated origin to its loss of self at the river, the creek was always the same, yet ever changing. Fast and turbulent in a straight run here, it was oxbowed, deep, and deceptively placid there. The water was often lightly frozen along one stretch, ice-crusted at the banks along another, and wide open at still another. The speed of its race to the river, the swirls of its deep eddies, and the warmth lingering from its beginnings combined to thwart the deathly cold of January.

When the man and his dog—I'll call them John and Shadow— left the house in the predawn on that early January morning, the mercury in the garage thermometer was buried near its base. Cold enough, John decided, that the exact temperature wasn't relevant.

Cold enough that common sense dictated he and the Labrador walk back into the house and curl up in the warm beds they had just left. Cold enough, a fleeting thought told him to be dangerous. But John brushed aside the concern and loaded the Lab into the rear of his Bronco.

Thirty minutes later, he pulled into a wide spot on a dirt road and parked next to his hunting partner's truck. He rolled down the thick-frosted window, looked at Steve, and asked, unceremoniously, "You sure you want to go out? This is serious weather."

"There are mallards all over the creek," Steve answered in a way that left no doubt about what he wanted. "Something just spooked a bunch," he added, poking a gloved finger toward the white wall of mist hanging over the water. "Must have been a hundred of them jumped straight up, then went right back down. It won't take us an hour to get limits. We've done it before."

"Not in this kind of cold," John said, looking hard at his impetuous best friend, who was not known for sound judgment. He head-gestured at the dog crate in the back of the Bronco. "I'm worried about Shadow."

"I would've brought Brownie," Steve said, by way of an answer, his breath flowing out of the window in clouds, "but he's got a dinged-up foot. Anyway, Shadow's a tough dog; he can handle it. We'll be jump-shooting these birds, and that's different than a wet dog freezing in a blind. Come on over here and have some coffee, then we'll get going."

The thin light of the new morning did nothing to ease the cold. Quite the opposite, John thought as he released Shadow from his crate; an odd breeze had come with the dawn, swirling the deep powdery snow on the ground and fingering into every fold of clothing that wasn't buttoned tight. Shadow jumped from the Bronco's tailgate and hit the snow sitting, looking up at his owner, waiting to be released. At a finger snap, the dog leaped away, kicking up snow. He made a couple of full-speed turns around the trucks, marked the tires, then returned to John's side. He had a grizzled, salt-and-pepper look from the snow on his head and back—snow that couldn't melt.

The three of them walked slowly, quietly, across a meadow toward the bank of mist that overhung the creek. When they reached the water, each of them took positions that showed they had played the game before. Shadow worked the bank about fifteen yards in front of the men; John walked behind him at the creek's edge while Steve stayed twenty yards out in the meadow for ducks that swung in that direction. They had agreed to keep Shadow out of the water by shooting birds over land as much as possible.

The black dog had disappeared into the mist. They heard splashing, quacks, then a flurry of wingbeats. Two of the eight mallards that lifted from the creek peeled low and straight over Steve's head. He got them both going away at the same time Shadow emerged from the water and delivered a wing-tipped drake to John, who hadn't shot. The big retriever found both of Steve's mallards, which had tumbled deep into a drift of fluffy powder. The dog was soaking wet and had iced up almost immediately.

Over the next two hundred yards of creek, Shadow dug out two more crippled drakes and a dead hen from beneath the bank. Apparently, a dogless hunter had shot the creek a day or two before. John had yet to fire his gun, but Steve had wounded a third mallard that, when hit, arced backward, dropped into a deep oxbow, and had to be chased down.

Despite their best intentions, Shadow had been in the water for most of the forty-five minutes they had hunted. His body was completely armored in a coat of ice that weighed him down and rattled when he moved or tried to shake it off.

John called the dog to him and worked on the ice, removing as much of it as he could from the dog's chest and belly. "Maybe you ought to leave it on him," Steve said. "It probably keeps him warm."

"Don't bet on it," John answered sharply. He continued to pull and crush the layers and clumps of ice that covered all but the Lab's muzzle and lower legs. "I'm just about to call it quits," John said, without looking at his friend. "The chill factor must be forty below. It's too cold for him. I'm freezing myself."

The breeze, unusual that early in the morning, had picked up and was streaming straight down the valley floor. It was also breaking up the clouds of mist above the creek, a point that was not lost on Steve.

"Let's give it a few more minutes. We can see the creek now and pick our shots. Besides, look at your dog. He's ready to go." Shadow was sitting and staring at John waiting to be sent out to hunt.

Looking down at the ice-laden Lab, John said, "Just because a dog has heart—and Shadow has a lot—doesn't mean he's got the brains to figure out when to quit. You know that." Then, reluctantly caving in to his friend's persistence, he added, "Okay, a few more minutes."

John should have looked in his dog's eyes; he should have studied them closely. They would have told him that Shadow wasn't "ready to go," that he wasn't even there entirely. The dog's eyes would have announced that he was unraveling in the cold.

Indeed, "a few more minutes" and another water chase during a retrieve were all that it took for the Lab to come apart completely. He could barely climb the creek bank. When he reached land, he dropped the duck and simply stood there. Shivers and tremors rippled down his body. When he tried to walk, he wobbled from side to side, fell, then got up, stood with his legs spraddled, and stared blankly ahead.

John waded through the snow to reach Shadow and began to tear ice from his fur. "Give me a hand," he yelled at Steve, who was running to the dog. "Break off all you can, then rub his legs and chest while I cover him up," John took off a long, heavy woolen scarf and wound it around Shadow's chest, then removed his outer parka and wrapped the rest of the dog's body.

"Here, take my gun," John said in a voice thick as cold mud. "Run to the truck, turn the heat on high, and come back. I'll carry him as far as I can, then you'll have to take over."

Steve had grabbed both shotguns and was plowing his way to the vehicles before his friend finished talking. John picked up the Lab and cradled him tight against his chest. Tears froze around his eyes as he pushed and high-stepped rapidly through the powder, whispering, "I'm sorry, I'm sorry," in rhythm with each step.

"Let me have him," Steve ordered when he returned. "I'll carry him from here. Look, he's perked up from your body heat." Shadow raised his head toward John, licked his hand, and whined when Steve took him from his owner for the last several hundred yards to the trucks. Steve yelled over his shoulder into the swirling snow, "He's going to make it fine."

And he did. Within two anxiety-filled days, Shadow seemed normal. Nonetheless, John pampered him for a week. The Labrador recovered completely, but John didn't. He had been at the very threshold of losing Shadow, losing him not to weather that he couldn't control—not really—but to stupidity that he could have avoided. Never again, John vowed, would he knowingly put a dog in harm's way.

The creek flowed as before, dark and gun metal hued, unconcerned with the events that had unfolded on its white banks. The wind eased, then ceased its rush along the valley floor, but before it quit it erased the tracks of two men and a dog. Deep cold settled on the creek, and clouds of mist rose again like a wall over the water.

18
Working
Stiffs

As Labradors go, he wasn't much to look at. He was big—eighty pounds of muscle built from all-day, almost everyday rough shooting. Very rough shooting. He was mostly chest and shoulders, with hindquarters too light to match his front. Wide-set eyes, knowing and rich with expression, saved his head. When they stared at me, I could forget that the too-narrow muzzle in front of them could nearly fit down the mouth of a milk bottle.

Looks aside, he got the job done, every job that I asked of him—whether normal, oddball, or hair-raising. He was a blue-collar dog, an unalloyed working stiff.

I'm ashamed to admit it, but in those days I hunted everything that flew, ran, hopped, or swam. If an animal was edible or, often, just there, I was after it. And when I was hunting, which was the bulk of the time, so was this particular Lab.

During his life, he patterned, sprinted, dog-paddled, and low-crawled from sea level to tree line. He hunted a hodgepodge of game and varmints, and retrieved an outrageous assortment of prey. He worked in blizzards and on the fringes of hurricanes; he was with me—afoot and on horseback—in the unforgiving moistures, blaze of deserts, and the iron cold of high-mountain winters. He followed my frequently obsessive, and occasionally foolish, pursuits without hesitation or a hitch in his gait.

What this singular Labrador lacked in appearance, style, and—I admit—deeply embedded talent, he made up in brains, work ethic, and drive. These qualities caused him to follow me wherever I led him and to do what I asked of him when we got there. He was my first honest-to-God working stiff, and I've had a soft spot for the type ever since.

I mean dogs that are loyal to their owners but self-reliant; completely devoted but independent when necessary; good at solving problems but lacking even a hint of the renegade. In the depths of their lineage, which may or may not be impressive, these dogs were bred for function. As a result, they perhaps lost a measure of physical beauty, but they gained a greater purpose. Few of them have much formal education; they don't seem to need it. Fewer still own advanced degrees, but these individuals excel at their jobs. However, beneath their trained-in, formalized polish, there remain strong suggestions of the working stiff.

A while back, a friend of mine lost one of the all-around finest springer spaniels I've seen. From big-time field trial winner to first-class wild bird hunter, this dog had it all. Intelligence, talent, and a flair for showmanship came together in this spaniel, but I believe that in his heart this wonderful dog was a working stiff. And that made him superior. At bottom, he had what each of these dogs brings to its work: competence, confidence, and a determination to give an honest day's effort to its employer.

Working stiffs don't sit down on the job because the day is too hot or too cold, or because the briars are too sharp or the marsh is covered with leg-bruising skim ice. They don't quit when their feet are sore, their tail-tips are bloody, or their bellies are brush-abraded red. It's up to the boss to say, "Enough," on waterless afternoons or when pads are cut or backs are wire gouged. Such dogs aren't fussy, self-absorbed prima donnas who sulk or slink back to the truck after a reprimand. Show them what's needed, and they get it done without complaint.

Over the course of a life with gun dogs, I've been lucky to own a couple of working stiffs. One of them, oddly enough, was a golden retriever who belied the standard image of the breed as silken-hairdo, preppy pooches fit only to ride in the front seat of Mercedes sedans, enrollee to fashionable beauty salons. He was an old-style golden, out of European breeding, with a short, wavy, richly-hued coat that turned back any weather. This was a working dog—powerful and impervious to hardship with a body and mind more akin to those of a Chesapeake Bay retriever than a golden.

But he was a working dog born too late. His nature and skills were less suited to the day-here, day-there schedule of the modern hunter than to the routine of market gunners in the last century: hunt all day, eat a bear's ration at night, sleep under the duck boat regardless of weather, guard the decoys and gear, then be up in the dark of morning to hunt again. And when the ducks quit flying, a retriever had to move to upland game, if that was the program. Then the dog would repeat it all the next day and the next.

Finesse was not part of my gold's makeup. His life was the hunt—and the quarry at the end of it—and he would run over or through anything to get to that game. Going around an obstacle never occurred to him. If that obstacle happened to be a half-ton of stubborn moose that needed facing down because it stood between him and a grouse, so be it.

Same thing with a pod of seals bent on mugging him for the sea duck he was retrieving from an icy tidal river. Blended with the background tumble of light surf and seal barks I heard a deep, toothy snarl oozing around the duck he refused to drop. Like many working stiffs, he had the élan and raw courage of a street fighter beset by a pack of pesky hooligans.

In the same vein as my blue-collar Lab, the golden had nothing elegant about him. Neither dog was a fast, flashy worker whose style compelled admiration, who burned up cover or churned water on a retrieve. Neither dog tolerated foolishness from crippled birds. Each ran them down and delivered them to hand in a workmanlike way. And woe betide the head of a goose or pheasant that pecked, wing-banged, or spurred these dogs. Only the head, mind you. I never received a body-damaged bird— out of hundreds—from either dog.

Occasionally, there are dogs who show at a glance whether or not they are working stiffs. As a case in point, I think back to one of my springer spaniels. He was a very nice, finely bred dog, but his style conjured the image of a stuffy British lord in an exclusive club, sipping rare scotch between methodical puffs on a meerschaum pipe.

During the same time frame, another of my springers— equally well-bred—was instantly identifiable as a keg-of-beer, elbows-on-the-bar, unfiltered-cigarettes sort of dog who was ready to run at life as it came to him. Early on, this spaniel was scatterbrained, not quite steady enough to be tagged as a real working stiff. But I kept up my hopes for him, and he made the grade. It's not hard to guess which of the two springers—"Rare Scotch" or "Keg of Beer"—turned out to be the better gun dog.

Working stiffs are underrated. The blue-collar label bears the stigma that it is not good to labor honestly for a living, to work without fuss or flash. So what if some of these dogs aren't always exciting? So what if they don't raise blood pressures because their performances are more businesslike than scintillating? So what if some of them aren't especially good looking or are rough around the edges? It's easy to be pretty. To be pretty good is another matter.

Working stiffs, the real article, aren't dilettantes who dabble in the gun-dog game when the mood strikes them. Like my Labrador who wasn't much to look at, they always show up for work and get their jobs done right.

19
Anything But Ordinary

"There are two kinds of hunting:" wrote Aldo Leopold in his classic book, *A Sand County Almanac*, "ordinary hunting and ruffed grouse hunting."

Leopold's famous line is another way of saying that ruffed grouse require thought. Indeed, everything about them demands attention. They are not casual birds and, likewise, they are not for casual hunters. Nor are they for shooters. Doves are the birds for those who like to pull triggers; grouse are not. Mostly, what we do with a grouse gun is load it, carry it, and unload it. Grouse *hunting* is measured by the mile and by the hour, while grouse *shooting*, when it occurs, is a matter of yards and pieces of seconds.

The hunting of grouse involves more wit and perception than luck, more motion than productivity, more reaction than action, more life than death.

Grouse are birds of the mind—wild birds not only of the edge but on the edge. Their hair-trigger attitudes are laced with paranoia, a deep suspicion of every motion and noise not of their own making. All of which means that grouse hunting is a tactical exercise comprising much more than occasional upland ramblings on clean and weightless October days. But, from another angle, those hunts under a perfect sun that glistens the webs of spiders and eases the passage of browning ferns are also very much a part of it. Grouse make you consider where you walk and what you see.

 Proper grouse hunting is done with a dog. Always. To do otherwise is to lose the magic of the bird, of how and where it lives. A covert with birds, a hunter, and a gun—but no dog— is incomplete, a formula lacking a critical component. But, just any dog won't do.

Aldo Leopold's defining statement on grouse hunting has a corollary in gun dogs. Few who know this bird would deny that there are also two kinds of dogs: ordinary dogs and ruffed-grouse dogs. Grouse demand at least as much from dogs as they do from hunters, and they usually demand much more. Which is the very reason why acceptable grouse dogs are uncommon, and consistently fine performers are rare. Given the bird, that seems appropriate.

Serious grouse hunters are perfectionists at the top of their game. The best are individuals who pursue the bird for the detailed quality of the hunt, which translates into the beauty of bird and dog performance without concern for a death at the end. Nowhere in the grouse hunter's code of personal conduct afield is it written that gaining this beauty requires dead birds.

Grouse hunters and grouse dogs will never have their fire for the chase dampened by domestication and tameness. Their bird is—and will remain—forever wild. And, come autumn, the quest for this wildness is a better reason than most to get up in the morning and watch a dawn break, then cut loose a grouse dog for an anything-but-ordinary hunt.

*   *   *

Sunlight streamed through the birches at a sharp, early-morning angle. It danced on limbs and trunks before ricocheting off snowy bark and dropping earthward to puddle on fallen leaves. The air was clear and still and soft enough for motes of dust to hang as free as bird songs in the beams of sun.

At the edge of the birch stand, the creamy whiteness was thinned by upright lines of aspen gray and scattered triangles of pine green that, in turn, faded downward into a rich purple sprawl of blackberries. Here, a soft breeze rustled in harmony with the sliding murmur of a creek threading its way toward a shallow backwater that ballooned from a river. A great blue heron stood in the shallows, tethered by the leg to his own reflection.

The bird turned his head at a quickening of the downsloping air, listened, then cut his bond with the water and lifted across the river to the safety of the opposite bank. The heron made his ungainly landing at the same moment the setter broke from the woods on the far side of the backwater. Patches of hunter-orange vest showed through the trees not far behind the dog. The man emerged from the trees and sat on a rock at the water's edge, waiting for the dog to drink and soak himself cool.

Droplets of water and tiny, sunbeamed prisms of mist filled the air around the setter as violent shakes ran the length of its white and black-dappled coat. Then the leggy dog trotted to the hunter's side. "We'll go in a minute," the man said, stroking the wet fur. "We need to think how to do this right," he added, unconsciously head-gesturing toward the birches.

They had been together six years and for the last four of those years man and dog had hunted the large covert up from the backwater. But the man always stopped and considered "how to do this right" each time he worked the area. And the setter, following his owner's lead, sat quietly, as though he too was assessing the wind, moisture, and time of day, and pondering the imponderables of exactly where a ruffed grouse would be at that moment.

The setter's cast away from the backwater took them along

the riverbank, led them through a stretch of alders, then angled back toward the tangled growth of berries. Light bell sounds kept dog and hunter in touch, though for grouse covers the setter ran big, wide, and easy, his mouth open as if he was drinking the wind. The dog ran precisely as the man trained him to run: at bell range, fast over earth that was his, stopping only when the breeze swirled in confusion, or when he winded grouse.

It was the setter's business to find birds, then the man's to find the setter. It was the grouse's job to outwit them both. At bottom, it was a question of how often skill, experience, and thought can get the better of skittish paranoia and a complete knowledge of home ground.

Near the thread of water, on the slope where aspens and berries bowed to each other, the setter did its job. The hunter turned and moved toward the final jangle of the bell, looking for white amid the hues of covert color. Confidence in the setter showed in the man's steady but unrushed pace. The dog would be where the bell sounded last, at the point where he had made game.

The hunter worked up the slope, skirted the dense edge of berry brambles, and eased into the aspen clusters. He weaved between two pines, then saw the setter's tail arcing above a jumble of scrub growth. Three side steps revealed the dog locked up hard and staring, narrow-eyed, straight at the hunter, twenty yards away. That left the bird pinned in a sunny aspen glade—with nowhere to go but up—between himself and the bright image of the dog. "Perfect," the man whispered. "Just perfect."

He took two steps forward, eyes focused above the setter, and the grouse flushed low and straight, just clearing the scrub growth. Not in front of the hunter, where it should have been, but behind him from under one of the pines he had passed.

And the savvy bird was gone, screened by the tree, before the pine duff settled beneath its explosive exit, before the hunter could turn and swing on the hint of departing shadow.

A tap on the head released the setter. "Gone," the man said a moment later, telling the dog what it already knew. He kneeled in the scrub and called the dog to him. "You were perfect," he said, smiling wide at the setter and scratching a black ear. Then he laughed into the aspens, immensely pleased with both dog and bird. He offered a full hand salute and yelled down the flight line of the departed grouse, "Nice work. I'll see you again."

*　　*　　*

To be sure, ruffed grouse require thought. When we think that we have them, we usually don't. When we think that a bird is ours for the shooting, it usually isn't. Even the uncommonly fine work of a legitimate grouse dog guarantees nothing—at least nothing but opportunity here and there. And that's the way it should be with a bird that has transcended the realm of ordinary hunting.

20

Climbing to High Ground

The young man braked the car sharply, twisted the wheel hard left, then eased off the highway onto a dirt road. He had nearly missed the turn. For the last few miles, what he saw through the windshield seemed different than what he remembered. The whole of it was still there, but in a way that he couldn't grip, something had changed since he'd been gone. Distracted by a vague separation from the familiar, he had almost driven past the road and the crimson spread of its landmark maple.

He followed the narrowing dirt track up a long slope that topped out in a growth of old gnarled apple trees, then dead-ended against the darkness of a granite bluff. He rolled down the window and inhaled morning air. His eyes roamed across the rock face to the overgrown trail that switchbacked upward through boulders that rose like the tumbled emplacements of a fallen fortress. For a full minute, he sat still, breathing deeply, trying to shake the feeling that he was missing-in-action in his own life story. Then, he clenched his hands around the steering wheel, closed his eyes, and leaned forward to rest his forehead on the wheel's thin rim.

Fifteen hours before, he had walked out of a stark building, changed clothes in the sweltering parking lot, pitched his gear onto the car's back seat, and left without ceremony. He had driven through the night, gradually leaving the clinging heat and oppression behind him, moving northward toward the freedom of unalloyed autumn. He had pushed the car steadily, staring down the pencil beams of his vehicle's headlights; begrudging stops for gas, coffee, and other necessities; spurred by a need to put distance between himself and where he had been.

Now, parked in the apple trees, he slid back in the seat, turned abruptly, and reached into the rear of the car. He shoved aside the bulge of a canvas duffel with his name stenciled in faded black letters below the hand grip. Amid the toss of baggage and discarded clothing, he found a small, sunbleached pack that he swung onto the front seat, then flipped open the top and shoved in a thermos of coffee. He got out of the car, eased the door shut with a soft click, and walked to the bluff, where the trail began its climb to high ground.

A ruffed grouse thundered up from under his feet, in the poplars at the bluff's base. The bird's explosive flush fractured the stillness and startled him badly. "Damn," he muttered under his breath. "Damn." He took a step forward and two more came out of the poplars. His heart tightened again, but this time in a good way. "Young birds," he said aloud, and sensed old feelings begin to flow as he watched the grouse arc into the sunlight gathering at the orchard's far end.

The trail was thin and curled against the slope, between granite outcroppings, like the lash of a whip. It wasn't far to the bluff's plateau—less than two hundred yards—but it was a steep climb, nearly straight up in one spot, and he was breathing hard when he came out of the boulders. The top was as he remembered it: barren of vegetation except for sprawls of ground-hugging junipers, coarse-bladed grasses, and mosses and lichens that crawled out of deep crevices and tendrilled to daylight over rough stone.

There was a rock wall, whose purpose no one remembered, that ran along the edge of the bluff where it sloped downward to the valley floor. Many times, in what now seemed like another life, he had sat on the slope, his back against the wall, with a shotgun broken across his lap. Then, his arm had been around an English setter, their faces catching the wind, each doing different things with what came to them over the miles. He had never climbed the high bluff to hunt; other than the occasional raven and old smart whitetail buck, no animals used it. Then, as now, he came for an uncluttered view of where he had been and for a sense of where he might be going.

The sun had lifted well above the horizon, bathing the bluff in a salmon hue, reconfiguring the severe look of the granite and gentling its color from shadowy black to mottled gray. Far out over the valley, a turkey vulture circled with locked wings, spiraling wide and upward on rising thermals.

The young man stepped over a low spot in the wall, walked a few steps along it, unshouldered his pack, and sat on the grass, already brittled by frost. He looked down the slope, taking in the sweep of a valley that was smaller, somehow, than his mind's eye recalled. He followed the serpentine contortions of the river and its surrounding color before he came to the charred darkness of the land that had burned the same year he had left. The burn was one of the few things he could remember from that year, at least with any precision.

Below him, blackened stumps and ragged tree trunks rose starkly out of the firm beginnings of regrowth. A firebreak had stopped the blaze well before it reached the river. Beyond that break, along the river bottom, he could see the dull gray greens of mature alders and the poor yellows of autumn birch and scrub willow. Across the river were more alders on land that terraced upward in bright stands of maples, oaks, and poplars.

His eyes caught movement among the alders, but the distance was too great for detail. He reached into the small pack and pulled out binoculars—big and powerful, heavy enough to need support for clear vision. From habit, he bent his knees and dug his elbows into his thighs for a prop, as if he was stabilizing a rifle for a long shot. The river bottom leaped toward him—out of focus at first, indistinct, then sharpening with slow adjustment until he could make out the wrinkled shapes of the leaves.

He saw the dog first—a mostly white setter weaving systematically through the long run of alders. Fluttering leaves told him that the dog was hunting an angling crosswind. And he was doing it thoroughly, covering ground at medium speed, not over casting, but reaching out just far enough before cutting back on a diagonal to put the wind in his nose. Crosswinds prevailed in that covert, the young man remembered, coming off the river in confusing swirls that tested a dog's experience and savvy. From what he could see, the setter was handling the alders well, hunting them smoothly and without a hitch.

He felt a quick catch in his throat, almost as though he was admiring the work of his own setter but in an oddly impersonal way—without involvement, without the deep, uncluttered enjoyment that he always found in the sight of a fine gun dog. Maybe, he thought, if he could hear the clangs of the big cowbell that hung from the dog's collar he would shed his sense of detachment; maybe that simple sound would offer him a connection to the solid reality of the English setter by the river.

Then he saw the hunter walking the alder run's center, along a thread of spring water. Something about the man looked familiar, but his features were obscured. Maybe it was the loose, stalking way he moved, the way of tall, angular men. Neither graceful nor gangling, it was the way a friend had once described his own walk. The hunter stopped and cocked his head slightly, like a man with damaged hearing trying to catch a sound. Then he moved on, high-stepping quickly through fallen alders and looking from side to side.

The dog stood out, even at a distance, etched clearly against alder green and the deep brown of the leaf-littered bottom. What looked to be buff-orange ticking dotted the setter's head and rump. His front legs were bent, his head low and turned to the side, as he leaned into the point. His tail was straight up. The young man imagined the dog's flanks quivering and the eyes, now irrelevant, narrowing to almost closed and the brownish nostrils flaring to pull in all the bird had to give.

He watched the hunter walk steadily up the run, saw him pinpoint the dog, pause, and glance around at the cover. He watched the man move in on the setter, slide off to the dog's side, and circle to his front. The woodcock flushed up into the limbs of the alders, rose above them, then twisted and sideslipped toward the river.

From the bluff, through the far-sighted binoculars, the scene drifted into slow-motion, going frame by frame, each one exact and defined: The familiar hunter raising his shotgun and poking it at the bird; the dog steady but watching the flight; the clean collapse of the woodcock followed by the distance-softened bump of the shot; the signal for the retrieve; then the delivery.

It was the last act that clutched the young man's heart.

When the setter brought in the woodcock, he sat in front of the hunter, head up and waiting. The man laid his shotgun on the ground, straightened, held his vest pocket open, and patted his chest with his other hand. The setter reared on his hind legs, put his paws on the man's chest, and dropped the bird into the pocket. Man and dog stood together, fixed in a too-private embrace, looking into each other's eyes, before the hunter gripped the dog's head with both hands and appeared to say something to him.

The young man slowly lowered the binoculars, still staring blankly in the alder run's direction. "Christ," he said very softly. "Ah, Christ."

He put the glasses back into the pack, carefully, taking out the thermos, then a pint of bourbon. He poured the thermos top full of the now cool, oily-muddy coffee and set it on the stone wall. He opened the bourbon, had a long pull off the bottle, and chased it with the coffee. Not fit to drink, he decided; it just ruined the whiskey's bite. A cigarette would have to do.

Tobacco smoke swirled away from him on an upslope breeze. It was the best cigarette he'd ever tasted. Another bourbon swallow burned him all the way down, with a good, cleansing, cauterizing heat that washed straight into his gut. His eyes were moist—from the sear of the whiskey, he told himself. Until he blinked away the wetness, he felt that he was seeing the world through the blur of rain-washed windows.

The sun was angled high and bright, beaming onto the side of his head. A rising wind fingered his short hair, tousling it a bit just as it ruffled the coarse grass of the slope. He looked down the valley—over the burn, now brighter under sunlight; across the wide ribbon of river; and into the alders. He lingered on the alder run for just a moment, then turned and stubbed out his smoke. He knew he'd be back. He was young, and so was the autumn.

He stretched full length on the slope. Before he draped an arm over his eyes, he glimpsed a tattering of thin clouds that marred an otherwise immaculate horizon. Then he slept.

21
Final Day

The day felt new, crisp, clear. And the air had an edge to it—reminiscent, in part, of mid-autumn, though in greater part suggestive of approaching winter. So, too, were the enduring patches of snow. Crusty leftovers from an early storm, they signaled the end of fall and offered a hint of what was to come.

No wind rustled the covert, but a few lingering, shriveled yellow leaves drifted quietly off aspens that flanked a clearing, which, in turn, butted against the shadows of a pine stand near the river. The aspens, along with the birches, alders and a few maples, had long since punched the seasonal time clock and cloaked the covert floor with their fading beauty.

Across the river, dark flocks of crows swept the sky and dropped noisily to earth to glean the remains of a long-harvested cornfield. Crow squabblings carried well on the clean, dry air and mixed with the occasional, guttural croaks of solitary ravens down from hard weather to the north. The thick, raucous noise flowed from the field, across the width of water, and through the pines, where it seemed to pause then break into distinct pieces over the hunter and his dog.

They were sitting, both of them, on a massive stump, the decaying remnant of a tree logged before most living memories. The wood had been moldering for unrelenting decades, eroding slowly under a green mat of moss. A large cock grouse was lying on one side of the stump with its head draped gently over the edge. Even in death, the grouse retained the grace that was, in part, a measure of its life.

The man had shaken the bird to fluff its feathers and to spread its metallic ruff and wide-banded tail before laying it down where he could glance at it from time to time, knowing it was the year's last grouse. A few days remained of the season, but he would not shoot again. He had hunted enough during the past months, and he knew, as well, that he would not top the admirable bird stretched near him on the moss.

Thirty minutes earlier, the setter had locked up fifteen yards from a lightening-fractured pine, just as she had done on four other hunts in that covert during the season. There had been no shot on the first two flushes out of the knocked-down pine, and the man had missed cleanly on the last two. Although the grouse did something different on each flush, intuition fired by long experience told the hunter it was the same, savvy bird.

Now he could see the setter's nostrils flaring in the still air, seeking a more convincing bead on the grouse. She took two stiff-legged and almost imperceptible steps forward, shifted her head slightly to the left, and stopped. Just to her front, the hunter held up his flattened palm and pushed it toward her in a silent command to "Whoa" right where she stood. All the dog could tell him was that the elusive bird was somewhere within the forty feet of jumbled, broken pine.

The man circled the edge, dead branches snapping underfoot and limbs scraping his brush pants. Periodically, he stopped abruptly, then moved again. He was on the back side of the pine, directly opposite the setter, when the high-strung grouse, caught between the hunter's deliberate noise and the dog's silent presence, erupted from under the tree's broad trunk.

Dry needles and wet snow scattered along the bird's path as it blew out low, hitting branches and beating through shrubs crushed by the pine's fall. The grouse arrowed straight at the dog, not five feet off the ground, once again using the pine to cover his escape. Until he was in front of the setter. Then he veered, virtually reversing direction, almost tumbling in the air like a woodcock. Then the bird raced away from the dog and back over the blowdown, barely clearing its up-thrust limbs—and the hunter on its far side. If the flustered man had grabbed his hat, he could have swatted the grouse with it.

The bird's tactic almost worked. Pivoting too rapidly, trying to follow the fast-winging grouse, and playing catch-up with the swing of his gun, the man missed a straightaway shot with his first barrel. There was nothing evasive, now, in the bird's flight. It was all speed, downslope, as the grouse made for the swath of pines lining the riverbank. And that was where the hunter's second barrel caught him, at thirty-five yards, in a tumble of feathers. The man marked the rough position of the fall, then walked around the old pine to his setter. He spent a moment stroking her, telling her she was a fine, steady dog. He heeled her to the point of his shot and released her on a line to retrieve the grouse.

When the dog placed the cock bird in his hand, the hunter looked closely at its perfection and thought about the point, the singular flush, the shot, the retrieve, the wholeness of it all. It was then that he knew this bird would finish their season. What had just taken place was impossible to surpass, and almost impossible to match, but would quite likely have its finality diminished if he hunted on and encountered a lesser bird. For this year, he declared his own last day, one that would remain intact in his mind's eye. Let next season bring what it would.

He sat on the moss-cushioned stump with an arm around

the setter, scratching her ear. He stared through the trees at the river's swirling, gunmetal surface and thought how cold and heavy the water appeared, how winterish it looked with the crows carrying on in the adjacent cornfield, how it contrasted with the autumn-like clarity of the day. The river had the sad look of an entity forever on the move, while the covert seemed placid, content to end the season and rest in winter's coming lockup.

The man began talking to his setter in one of those meaningless monologues that, oddly, both hunters and dogs enjoy. She turned her head to listen to the man, and he saw a grouse breast feather stuck in the corner of her mouth. He reached over to pluck it off, then pondered for a moment and decided the feather belonged where it was. If the dog tired of it, she'd paw the feather away. Otherwise it would simply drop off and float to earth like a last aspen leaf in a clear, windless covert.

Until then, the feather, too, was part of the final day's symmetry.

Part III

The Last Years

The old dog barks backward without getting up.
I can remember when he was a pup.
—Robert Frost

22
One Hundred Percent

"My Brittany is nine years old and slowing down," the speaker told the sizable audience at the gun-dog seminar. "I'll use him the rest of this fall," he added casually, as if he was talking about a worn-out shotgun. "But when bird season ends, I'll put him down."

One listener thought he had misunderstood the speaker's intent and asked, "Did I hear you right? You're going to euthanize your Brittany next month?" Then he asked, "Why? Does the dog have a health problem that can't be treated?"

"There's nothing wrong with him," the speaker answered, missing the question's point. "But I don't want an old dog that can't give me 100 percent in the field. It's a waste of my time."

After a pause, the listener said, "Rather than destroy your Britt, why not give him to someone who would enjoy a few years of hunting with a fully trained, slower-working dog. I'll bet there are people in this audience who know the value of an older dog and would love to have yours."

At least a half-dozen hands shot into the air.

Eventually, we all get old. The weight of time presses on dogs in much the same fashion that it presses on people, though age and physical decline strike canines disproportionately fast relative to humans. Which is another way of saying that hunters have about five or six seasons to benefit from a dog at its maturational and physical peak. Before those middle years arrive, the animal is a developing youngster; beyond them the dog is elderly. Given that mini-span of prime seasons, it makes sense to realistically maximize what remains of the lives of our aging gun dogs and our times with them.

And these can be very good times.

An older dog is quite capable of giving 100 percent, but he'll offer such full measure in a different, tempered style. The meaning of 100 percent remains the same; only the context in which it is given has been altered. Whether in a canine or a human, it seems to me that age is best thought in terms of change and shifting expectations, not in terms of negatives such as lost or wasted time.

Indeed, hunting with a healthy, older dog can be downright enjoyable. His physical skills may be sliding, the slash-and-dash style of his youth may be gone, and the excitement of watching him in top form, running on the bare edge of control may be just a memory. But instead, you get a heightened focus and concentration, an economy of motion, a regulation of pace, a deliberation of intent.

About half my life ago, I helped a neighbor and his eighty-two-year-old father load alfalfa from several sections of pasture. I was young and in good condition, and I tossed bales like a dervish. But by midmorning on the first day, I was sucking wind and nearly out of gas. The old man continued to move along slowly, methodically hoisting fifty-pound bales and showing little sign of the effort.

I was bent at the waist, catching my breath, when he walked over to me and said, "We're not going to get this done in an hour or a day, so slow down. In the long run, you'll move just as many bales, and you'll be alive at week's end."

He smiled, kindly man that he was, and added, "You remind me of that Labrador pup we have back at the house. He runs like hell for an hour and burns himself out. But he doesn't find any more pheasants than our old dog, who paces himself and is still on his feet when the hunt is over. Take it easy, and try to be an old dog."

From a slightly different angle, it is often the final years of a dog's active life that hunters come to treasure the most. I can't remember how many times I've heard people say something like, "Old Rover, here, has turned into a pretty good dog over the past couple of seasons. You should have seen him a while back; he was a hawk-wild, out-of-control bird chaser. For six or seven years, he thought his name was "Get-in-here-Rover-you-son-of-a-bitch," because that's all he heard. But he's a hell of a dog now. I guess all of my training finally sank in."

It usually turns out that Rover is ten or eleven years old. He became a "hell of a dog" not through training that "finally sank in" but by way of experience and the natural moderation that accompanies age.

But how old is *old?* When does a normal gun dog in good health turn the corner, passing from his middle years into old age? For whatever it's worth, veterinary research suggests that, on average, medium-sized to large dogs—categories that account for all the upland-bird and waterfowl breeds—become geriatric at nine to ten years of age. A less broad definition, but one that is equally vague, says that dogs are elderly when they begin to develop age-related problems.

In truth, there is no standard explanation of age, no satisfactory answer to the question: How old is *old?* Phrased another way, we don't know what *old* means in real terms. And perhaps that is best. The nebulous nature of age should keep us from mentally pigeonholing our dogs — or discarding them — on the basis of statistical averages. To be sure, dogs are as physically variable during their geriatric stage as they are in their youth or midlife.

A few years ago, several friends and I hunted quail behind an English pointer who was two weeks shy of his eighteenth birthday. His owner told us that the dog's sight wasn't great and that he couldn't hear a shotgun blast at ten feet. But the man said that for an old-timer, the pointer was in fair shape and could still hunt. He was apologetic in adding that after eighteen seasons together, he couldn't bring himself to leave the dog at home.

The man went on to talk about this pointer in some depth, then asked whether we minded if he let the dog run for a time. Of course we didn't mind.

The old dog wasn't going to win any field trials, but for an hour in the cool of morning and a half-hour in the late afternoon, he was all business and produced quail. Within the limits of his capabilities, he gave 100 percent.

I admired that eighteen-year-old pointer, but more to the issue, I admired his owner. Although the man had other bird dogs, he had not written off as a waste of time this pointer, who had been with him for his entire adult life. Euthanizing the dog hadn't occurred to him, nor had relegating the animal to a kennel until he finally died.

Rather, years earlier, the man had adjusted his expectations of the aging dog. He didn't look for the same level of effort or degree of vigor or type of performance that he had seen when the dog was young. He didn't run the pointer under rough conditions but judged each piece of cover by what he knew his dog could handle.

Most of all, I admired the man because he understood that to an old dog the quantity of its time in the field isn't important. Just being out there with its owner, its person, is what matters. This man readily acknowledged that while his pointer's body had changed, the depth of the animal's heart remained unaltered.

These days, when I see an older gun dog or hear a sportsman voicing concern that his hunting companion is "getting up there," I don't think about the owner of the nine-year-old Brittany that was slowing down—the small-minded owner who refused to understand the subtle qualities of the 100 percent his Britt still had to offer.

Rather, my mind flips back in time to the more inspiring image of a quail hunter following the measured steps of his eighteen-year-old pointer. Each in his own way, this man and his much-loved dog knew what giving 100 percent is all about.

23
Matched
Pairs

I liked the look of the man and his dog right off. We both had springer spaniels, so that was a piece of it. But there was something else.

Maybe it was the easy way they moved toward me, along the fringe of the covert's old road. Their style said "this is a nice pair," though it was nothing obvious like a greeting wave and a big smile, friendly words, or a wildly wagging tail. When I thought about them later and rehashed the details of our meeting, it was their aura of mutual contentment that hung in my mind. Both man and dog had the look of doing exactly what they wanted, each knowing that in the other he had the perfect partner.

In terms of years, they appeared past their peak, gray around the muzzle and at the same point in that final stretch of late middle age where they understood their goals and had a fair idea how to achieve them. Both were on the portly side, the products of good living. This was a matched brace of experienced trenchermen who enjoyed doing honest service to their respective bowls of chow. But underlying their heft was a hint of endurance that suggested these two could pace themselves and be where they intended, having done what they intended, at day's end.

The man's field manners, like those of his dog, spoke of

a good many seasons in bird covers. Before he reached me, he paused in the road, broke his shotgun, and dropped the shells into a side pocket of his hard-used vest. When he stopped to unload, the spaniel slid across the road and sat by his side. The man draped the double over his shoulder, muzzles to the rear, then walked to the log where my springer and I were sitting. His dog stayed heeled without a command.

"Afternoon," he said in the sort of smooth, modulated voice I had expected, perhaps hoped for. "Do you mind if a couple of tired old-timers share your seat for a while?" He brushed off a sugary sift of old snow, eased onto the log, sighed comfortably, and laid the shotgun across his lap. The springer was still glued to his leg. Although I had first seen them just minutes earlier, I knew this was the way they looked at home: the man in his favorite chair, the dog at his side, both of them relaxed and perfectly pleased with life at that moment.

I decided, as well, that we were a study in Type B and Type A personalities. The man radiated a sense of tranquillity that conventional wisdom identifies as coming only with considerable age. In reality, he was probably just ten or twelve years my senior. But he personified maturity, while I, on the other hand, fidgeted like a teenager, always seeking a nonexistent soft spot on the log, needing a break and at the same time wanting to move on.

Same thing with my springer. His light whines were borne on little puffs of chilled breath, and his plunked-down rear end sashayed in place, in sync with a tail that was fanning a half-circle in the ground cover of dead leaves. Looking down at the dog's barely contained motion, it occurred to me that we, too, were a matched pair.

The man and I talked of grouse and flushing dogs, and wondered out loud why we had never run into each other in this smallish covert, though we had both hunted it for a decade.

"What's doubly curious," he said, "is that both of us run springers." Indeed, it was unusual in a region that favors pointing dogs. We also discovered that our spaniels were English-bred relatives—cousins, as best we could figure out on the spot—though separated in age by years and in style by their natures.

"Look at them closely," the man said, gesturing at the dogs. "Once you get past the differences in age and weight"— he paused to glance at me and smile—"they're very similar." He was right. It was mainly the heft, the extra poundage on his springer, along with its complacency, that camouflaged the older but still fine-looking dog underneath. My spaniel was young, wraith-lean and thin-waisted, feral-looking, and impatient to move on.

"My needs have changed over the years," the man said slowly, leaning back against the thick remnant of a branch. "I used to love high-powered springers like yours—I still do as long as someone else owns them. I admit that there is nothing better to watch than a fast, hard-driving dog that knows his birds and his job. Particularly with pheasants. I suspect that I'd still get goose bumps behind a springer that burned up a field, went into the air grabbing for feathers, then hit the ground rock-steady."

I could almost see into his head, toward the past, as his mind's eye watched the hot-shot spaniels he used to love. "That's as good as dog work gets. Nothing better," he repeated. "But, these days, it's not what I want for grouse and woodcock."

A long cloud blotted out the sun, and a skin of gelid air dropped over the slope where we sat in its rush to the creek below. Without the sun's warming glow, the covert was transformed into shadowless late autumn, stark and darkly cold. The man didn't seem to notice the sudden temperature plunge. He went on talking and whittling slices off a pocket-sized slab of smoked beef—one slice for the dog, one for him.

"I retired early, about three years ago," he told me. "Now that I have plenty of time, I spend most of autumn in the woods. I don't hunt ducks at all anymore and rarely go after pheasants. I've switched entirely to grouse and woodcock, and maybe that's what changed my mind about fast-working springers. My last one was a good retriever and a solid pheasant dog—he died a couple of years ago at fourteen—but he looked choppy and out of place when I first started putting him down in thick cover. Some of it was his training and experience, but he never really adjusted to hunting timber. I had to rein him in and handle him too much, so neither of us had a good time. That's when I started thinking about speed."

"My age is probably part of it, too," he continued, "but I've been opting for slower, closer-working dogs for some years now—dogs that wouldn't cut it in open country. Mainly, I think it's my having the time to take hunting easy. I don't have to cover a lot of ground today, because there is always tomorrow and the next day. And I still move a good many birds during a season. I just stretch them out over more days."

He paused, offered the last sliver of beef to his spaniel, then added, "I'm not denying the facts of getting old and slowing down. At least I don't think I am. As much as I can look at it honestly, I enjoy the birds, the coverts, and my three springers—especially the two older dogs—more than ever." At that moment, the placid springer shifted position and laid his head on the man's leg. The dog looked up at him with those wonderful eyes unique to spaniels, as if in tacit agreement that life was just right.

The man and his springer struck me as an island of satisfaction in an often discontented sea of hunters and dogs. Their demeanor alone told me that they were not in the coverts to prove anything to anyone, least of all to themselves.

And it was unimportant whether the man's knowledge of his wants brought their styles together or whether they had fine-tuned their relationship until they found the perfect mesh.

The afternoon's cold thickened beyond what light clothing and sitting on a log could handle. The man and I decided that it was time to warm up. We shook hands, then heeled our springers in opposite directions to cast them off and finish the day's hunt, each pair at it's own pace—one fast, the other slower.

We parted company knowing that only one thing mattered —all four of us were having a good time in our own fashion.

24
The Labrador Letter

Dear Joe:

Remember me, Bill Jackson, from the years you worked in Idaho? It's been a good while—more than eight years—since we talked, so you may have to rewind your mental clock a bit to recall my name and who I am. Here's a memory jog that should help.

When you moved out of town, for a reassignment up north (to the backcountry, I believe it was), you gave me a two-year-old Labrador pup named Shade. As I remember, you could take only one dog with you and opted to keep a young setter. You knew Shade would have a good home with me, but more than that—as you said—you knew how much I fancied him during the times we hunted together when he was a youngster.

But "fancied" became the wrong word after the first couple of months he was with me. The fact is that I loved the dog more with every year that passed. Outside of my wife and kids, he was the best thing that ever happened to me.

And now he is dead—I'll tell you about that in a minute—and I need your help to track down where he came from, where you got him, anything you know about his background. Not to replace him—he was unique in my mind—but to try to find another dog from a bloodline as close as possible to his. All I know is what is on his papers and what you told me when I took him: that Shade came from a deliberate breeding between a male and female owned by hunting partners of yours. Beyond that, I'm in the dark and have no clue how to contact these people.

First, the good part. I've had a fair number of Labradors over the past twenty years—decent dogs that were loyal, worked hard for me, and were good family members. You hunted behind one of them. They were all dogs that I cared about, but none of them approached Shade in any way.

You owned him during his beginning. You saw his potential and started developing it, but you couldn't foresee how deep that potential ran. (Thank goodness for that, or you wouldn't have given him to me.) You missed him when he began to blossom, then moved into the full flowering of his peak years. He was one of those dogs that looked promising —even good—as a young-ster and became fine as an adult. At least from my view, Shade did everything to perfection.

I wish you could have seen him work the river. Think back to those sections that we hunted, where the current is powerful and the ducks tuck into the small backwaters and fingers. Remember, too, the straight runs where geese lift off the corn-fields, then drop over the canyon rim to fly low along the water. I didn't keep a tally, but if Shade didn't pull two hundred birds a year from the river, I'll eat a raw goose—feet, feathers, and bill.

And pheasants? He flushed and fetched a bunch of birds for us as a pup, when you had him, but that was nothing compared to what he did—and how he did it—during the last eight years. He stayed steady, rarely lost a running bird, and never missed a mark no matter how long the retrieve. I even hunted him on valley quail along the river bluffs, ruffed grouse in the mountains, and sage grouse in the high desert. I've likely overworked this already, but Shade was a hell of a dog.

The dumbest thing I've ever done was my failing to breed him. I never found a female that I thought was good enough.

At least that's what I told myself. Though thinking back on it, and trying to be honest, I probably didn't look that hard; in truth, there are a lot of nice Labs in this part of the state. I suppose I was afraid that the pups wouldn't live up to Shade's standard. In that sense, I was avoiding any chance of disappointment rather than being mature enough to accept what turned out.

It could also be that Shade and I were so much a piece of each other's lives that I couldn't bring myself to share that relationship with another dog. Maybe that's it. And now I have nothing left from the best dog I'll ever own. Memories, yes, a mind full of them, but of Shade himself I have nothing.

And that brings me to the bad part. But first, I want to get something straight. Remember sitting in my workshop in those ratty chairs by the beer cooler, arguing about my letting my dogs run loose from time to time? Well, I heard what you were saying. Understand that Shade never ran free unless I was with him. He was so devoted that I doubt he would have left home anyway except to follow my truck, but it's important you understand that running loose had nothing to do with his death.

Whenever I was home, Shade lived inside with the rest of the family. During working hours, he stayed in a special kennel that I attached to the room off the workshop where I stored boats, boots, decoys, dog gear and the like—you've been in it. I put a two-way door from the kennel into the room so he could get under cover when the weather turned rough. But, more so than not—and regardless of the weather—he preferred the room to the kennel. He never used the fancy, cedar-filled bed I put down for him. He made a nest on a pile of camo netting. I guess it smelled right.

Anyway, about two months ago, I got home from work and didn't see Shade in his kennel. At the sound of my truck pulling in he'd always be sitting at the kennel door, tail thrashing, waiting to go wherever I was going. Then I called him. Nothing.

I found him in the storeroom, stretched over the camo pile with his head on one of my boots, which he'd yanked off the wall. He'd been dead several hours. From his appearance, it took a while for him to die. I still have nightmares about how bad, how twisted and stricken he looked lying in that room, surrounded by the things he loved.

I had my vet do a workup to find out what happened. Turns out it was one of the old coyote poisons that some ranchers still keep around and that a few still use, illegal or not. Shade also had two half-chewed, hard-boiled eggs in his stomach. Which means that someone drove up to my work-shop, tossed the poisoned eggs into the kennel, perhaps watched the dog eat them, then drove off.

Who or why? I have no idea and probably never will. But God help the sick son of a bitch if I find out. As far as I know, I don't have serious enemies—or at least none who would do something like that. Most people around here tend to be more direct. If they had a problem with me, it would be me they'd come after, not my dog. So, it seems, Shade was a target of pure meanness, the victim of an ugly act with no purpose other than to kill a dog. And that's the story of a wonderful partnership with a terrible ending.

I didn't intend to ramble on as I have, but in part I thought that you would want to know how Shade turned out and what ultimately happened to him. Mostly—though I know it's a long shot after all this time—I hope you can help me with some names and addresses of people who might have dogs from Shade's line. Thanks for staying with me through this letter.

I hope that you, your family, and your dogs are well.

Bill

25
Late
November

Ed was a pure ruffed-grouse hunter, and so was Blue, his thirteen-year-old English pointer. They didn't hunt the pheasants or quail that were a reasonable day's drive from their home. Nor did they hunt the woodcock that moved through their grouse coverts. Years before, Blue had learned to blow by those as if they were dickey-birds. No, this pair hunted only grouse—or partridge, in Ed's lingo.

"Blue here has never had anything but partridge shot over him," Ed said. He leaned over the log we were sitting on and patted the old dog's head. "Not a single bird. But he's worked a hell of a bunch of partridge. Likely, that's part of the reason he's been so good at finding them. I'll never own another like him."

Until that moment, it hadn't occurred to me to ask why he had named a liver-and-white dog Blue. "I was superstitious," Ed answered. "Earlier, I owned three other dogs named Blue, all of them first-class in different ways: a pointer, a Labrador, and my first one, a blue-heeler stock dog that just rode around with me.

"I liked this dog a lot when I saw him as a pup," he said, head-gesturing at the pointer, "so I gave him the name. It must have worked."

Indeed, for the seven seasons I had known Blue, the name

had worked to near perfection. And the magic was still working just before we sat on the log for a rest. Blue had been hunting a patch of mixed cover, casting out then bending back to use a cheek breeze. Spindly shanked, he was old-dog methodical in his search, moving at a slow, almost-walking trot that was the flip side of the dashing style of his prime years, those seasons when all coverts were his for the taking.

But when he locked up at the edge of a birch stand, his point had a rigid authority anchored in the certainty that a bird was in front of him, wedged with no escape between him and us. Ed made a nice shot on the grouse, then called Blue's name for the retrieve. The dog took two half-steps forward, angled his head low to the left, and froze again.

"Let's take a break," Ed said, after the pointer delivered both grouse. "Blue can't go much more than a half-hour at a time." He gave the dog a drink from his water bottle, then broke his shotgun and sat on the log. Blue nosed the birds for a minute, then went off a ways to lift his leg before he padded back and flopped onto a soft bed of club moss at Ed's feet. Then he rested his worn and bony head on Ed's boot. His chest rose and fell heavily, and his breath fluttered the frond of a dying fern. Ed reached down and rubbed a finger along a thin briar scratch that angled across Blue's nose.

"It's a sad thing for me to admit," Ed said abruptly, without any lead-in, "but I didn't pay attention to how fine Blue was until he started getting old. For a lot of years, I never gave it a thought. I just hunted him like he'd always be around." He paused for a moment before finishing his thought.

"You know, it's a rare dog that's first rate on partridge all of his life, but it's an even rarer dog that's just first rate in every way—like a close friend you'd describe as a gentleman. If Blue was human, I'd call him a gentleman."

Ed was still looking down and rubbing the dog's nose when he added in a low voice, "This is my last Blue. I'm not using the name again. It ends with this dog."

He straightened up, stretched his back, then picked up one of the grouse and fanned its tail. "I've shot a good many partridge over some pretty fair dogs that I cared a lot about, and it was always rough when they got old. But Blue is the worst. Much as I've tried during the last few years, I can't picture myself without him."

Ed paused and tipped back his hat. "I wish this dog could give out with his nose full of partridge at sundown on the l ast day of the best season we've had. But that isn't going to happen—it can't, now—so I'm not going to ruin thirteen great years by letting it stick in my head. We're going about business like we've always done. That's best, it seems to me, the way it should be. It just took me this long to understand it."

It wasn't like Ed to dwell on his troubles, even less so to talk about them. But he gave Blue another drink and a biscuit, and went on. "I finally figured out that if you worry about when a dog will die, you've already lost what time you have left with him. And you won't change a thing except make yourself—and likely your dog—miserable. If you think about your life without him, you've already let go of him; you've eased him out and turned him into a shadow that fades until you don't really see him anymore. And you've done it for yourself, to protect your own heart, not for the dog who has been a partner—and a friend—for a hell of long time. Hard as it is, I'm not going to turn Blue into a shadow."

At his name, the pointer raised his head and thumped his bone-ridged tail among the moss and ferns. "We'll go in a minute," Ed told him softly. "Stay down and rest a while longer."

Ed turned his head and looked down the log at me. "This

is Blue's last season in the field. I know that now, and I want him to have it for himself. I'm going to let him do whatever he can, whenever he is able, for as long as he can go without hurting himself. The birds we work this year will be just for him."

Ed let out a large breath, then with a throaty, "Let's go," he tapped Blue on the head. He stood and snapped his gun closed. After a couple of steps, he turned with a half-embarrassed look on his face and said, "Sorry. I didn't mean to lay that on you. It just fell out. I guess that I needed to hear myself say it."

I shrugged off his apology, then suggested we hit a nearby alder run where grouse might be tucked in along the cool earth of a streambed.

"That sounds about right," Ed agreed, smiling. "But do me a favor. If any woodcock are still around, leave them alone. Blue here is a partridge dog. Always has been, always will be."

26
A Fair Trade

The man, Jim, sat on the moss-covered surface of a crumbling oak stump whose once-hard edges had been worn down by the seasons. The remains of the oak's trunk lay close by, abandoned at the spot where it was felled by sawyers of another time. A stone wall trended down a slight slope at an angle to the decaying tree. Where the ground bottomed out, the wall turned sharply and paralleled a narrow alder run before its length of stones tumbled to nothing in a cluster of white pines.

From his familiar seat, Jim watched the earth brighten under vivid morning colors out of the eastern sky. On his westward side, a thin cloak of shadows still covered the slope. He pondered the covert's gentle, autumn beauty and allowed its subtle combination of sights and sounds and smells to open a door into his memory and ease him into a final recapitulation of the German short-haired pointer at his feet. The dog, though characteristically restless, was gaunt and enfeebled by the wasting impact of time.

The same shorthair had been with the man more than eight years before on another autumn morning—then, of course, the dog was a pup—when chance alone took them to this covert for the first time. Jim had turned right rather than left on an old road to nowhere. He had found the stone wall and had followed its rocky meanders east instead of west. Deep in the October woods, he had glimpsed a hint of emerald green that led him to the mossy stump and its toppled trunk, then on to the alders and the white pines. There Jim cut loose the wild-eyed pup—aptly named Jet—to free-hunt the thick cover. It was there, too, that he shot the young dog's first wild birds.

The man unsnapped the lead but held the lunging pup's collar for a moment before snapping his fingers and commanding, "Hie on." The seven-month-old shorthair rocketed for the alders. He was little more than a brown-and-white blur as he straight-lined through the cluttered center of the run for fifty yards, pivoted sharply in a full circle, and returned as fast as he had gone. Ten yards past the man, the pointer stopped as if he had bumped into an invisible wall. He took a short, tentative step, then lowered his head and leaned forward, frozen in time and place by an instinctive reaction to the heavy, narcotic scent of woodcock.

The man had done his homework before he bought the shorthair. The dog's breeding was unquestionably first-class, but something had occurred in the pup's developmental history that turned him into a definition of perpetual and often pointless motion. A veterinarian friend of Jim's had summed up Jet's case as, "the closest thing I've seen—at least in a well-bred hunting dog—to clinical hyperactivity. There aren't many options with a pup like this. You won't have an easy time with him." Then the vet added reluctantly, "On top of that, he's likely to wear himself out at a relatively young age."

Common sense—along with years of gun-dog experience—told Jim that his vet was right; the shorthair would probably be an endless nightmare. Although Jet showed no sign of being a temperamental rebel and was neither overbearing nor aggressive, he lacked the ability to stop moving and focus for more than a few seconds at a stretch. From that angle alone, the man knew that each rudiment of hunting for the gun would have to be drilled—and drilled hard—into the dog.

On the plus side of Jim's tally, Jet was one of the birdiest puppies he had ever seen. It hadn't taken the man long to discover that game birds were embedded in the shorthair's brain, a trait enhanced by the dog's excellent nose and strong pointing instinct. From his first trips into the woods, the pointer showed an uncanny ability to find birds. He seemed to intuitively distinguish between covers that held grouse and woodcock, and those that did not. Still, his idea of bird work was usually a rocketing, straight line.

Logic argued that the man should find the dog another home, but Jim had weighed Jet's hyperactivity against his raw bird-finding talent and had kept the pup. Many times over the years he had considered—and reconsidered—the wisdom of his choice, often from the comforting, sun-rich perspective of the mossy stump. The man acknowledged to himself that a major part of his decision to go ahead and train the pup was the need to see how the oddball hand that fate had dealt this dog—and in turn had given to him—would play out.

Although the shorthair commonly took Jim to the limits of patience and emotional endurance, in an odd way Jet's singular nature brought the two of them closer. Certainly, it taught the man things about dogs—and about his own personality—that he would not have otherwise discovered. Jet gave him, as well, some of the more memorable experiences of a lifetime with gun dogs. When hunts came together for the pointer, they did so in a big way. He was capable of virtuoso performances and offered them time and again over his eight full seasons in the field.

It was during December of the shorthair's sixth year when the man released him with the familiar finger snap and "Hie on." They had been standing at the oak stump—topped with close to a foot of new, powdery snow—looking out over the stark, white-cloaked earth. The land's subtleties and details were buried, but the man and his dog did not need them. They had hunted the covert many times since that first October morning.

The shorthair cleared the hidden stone wall in a leap and passed through the alder run without a glance—there would be no woodcock this late—on his way to the pines that might harbor grouse. The snow slowed Jet a bit as he skirted the conifers, then turned in a cloud of powder and darted under the snow-sagged limbs. Fifteen feet into the pines, the dog stopped abruptly and twisted his head to catch the high wind that sighed in the treetops before swirling down to the snowbound earth. The man heard the snorts of air pumping in and out of the shorthair's flared nostrils.

When the pointer zeroed in on the scent of the grouse tucked against a white pine's trunk, he locked up solidly at the tree's base. His head angled slightly skyward, and his eyes rolled further back as he waited for the flush and the shot. The dog had played this deep-winter game before—and he played it very well.

Maturity tempered Jet and—along with constant training—instilled a measure of self-control over his obsessive need to move. Midway along the wearing trail of time the shorthair had become a very decent gun dog, though Jim didn't fool himself on that issue. Jet should have been a magnum hunter by birthright, and likely he would have been but for the neurological disorder beyond his sway. But what the pointer had become was good enough. During the high-flying shorthair's active seasons, Jim had shot more grouse and woodcock over him than over any dog he had ever owned.

However, Jet paid a stiff price for a life of constant motion. By the end of his seventh season, the pointer was showing clear signs of being old before his time, and by his ninth year he was worn out and nearly finished. Even then—perhaps especially then—Jim continued to ask himself, "Did I do the right thing by not unloading the pup early on?" From a practical perspective, his answer was no; the years with Jet had been time consuming, monumentally frustrating, and often unpleasant for both of them.

But the man's heart presented a more genuine response. All things considered, especially in view of the deeper insights forced upon Jim by the shorthair's approaching end, a replay of their years together said to him that they had, indeed, been worth the effort. Jet had given his owner everything he could, as best he could give it, within the framework of his limitations. To expect anything more, the man knew, was unreasonable.

Jim's life with this bizarre German shorthair had been a walk on a wobbly, emotional tightrope. For nine years, the man's relationship with Jet had involved balancing periods of total loss against hard-won gains, of weighing motion without productivity against near-perfect bird work, of measuring unalloyed despair against unforgettable moments. The seasons they had together were marked by hardships that Jim would not want to repeat. But at least, he thought, they had played the game to its end, as fully and as honestly as they could.

Jim watched the pointer fidgeting at the base of the emerald-crowned stump. The dog's ever-going stub tail swept short arcs in the dusty litter, while his nose searched the air for whatever the breeze might bear. Jet rolled his head over his shoulder and glanced at the man, then whined and aimed his nose again at the alders. His internal overdrive was undiminished, yet held in check by years of discipline and—mainly—an exhausted, failing body.

The man, Jim, looked down at his dog, Jet, then rose from the mossy stump and knelt by him. He gripped the shorthair's thin, bony head lightly between his palms and stared long into the big and remarkably soft eyes.

Then, in a low voice, he said, "All in all, old fellow, what we've given each other has been a fair trade."

27
No New Tricks

When the man picked up the phone, the last thing he expected to hear was his closest friend abruptly saying, "I've found the perfect dog for Johnny—an older, fully trained Labrador."

"Hold on," John said in a low voice, cupping his hand around the phone's mouthpiece, then glancing over his shoulder at his son. "What are you talking about?"

"Just what I said. I've got the ideal dog for Johnny. You've been talking for over a year about getting him his own hunting dog; now you've got the chance. And a better one won't come along."

John Sr. walked into his study and shut the door. He didn't want his son hearing anything that might build hope but not work out. His longtime friend, Bob, however, wasn't the type to suggest something haphazard. Bob was also John's primary hunting partner, a veterinarian, and a dog man of considerable knowledge.

"Tell me more," John said, "and give me some details."

The upshot was that one of Bob's clients had to get rid of his Lab and was looking for an appropriate home. The man was willing to give the dog to the right person, especially if it was someone whom Bob recommended.

"This dog has been in my practice all of her life," Bob

went on in his rapid-fire fashion, "so I know her well. Her owner and I aren't close friends, but over the years I've hunted behind the dog maybe a half-dozen times. She's a bit on the small side for a Labrador, but she's in perfect health and has a sound, easygoing temperament. The dog is trained as an upland flusher, but she works waterfowl just as well. She's been loved and well cared for. Her owner is sick about giving her up, but because of personal difficulties that have nothing to do with the dog, he can't keep her. Incidentally, the man is a very competent trainer. You should really think hard about taking this dog."

John believed everything his friend had said. He knew that Bob cared for his son, Johnny, almost as much as he did, and in many ways saw himself as the boy's second father. If Bob said that the Labrador was a perfect dog for Johnny, then the fact of it was indisputable.

"Is she really that biddable?" John asked. "You know that as much as I travel these days, I don't have much time to teach Johnny how to handle his own dog."

"It's not a matter of his handling her; she doesn't need handling. When they're in the field, Johnny won't have to do anything but go where she goes. At this point, she knows a hell of a lot more than he does about birds and bird hunting. If he pays attention, she'll show him what he should know and give him what he needs. And he won't have to teach her a thing—no new tricks—in or out of the field."

"You're right," John Sr. said, "she sounds perfect, but you haven't mentioned her age."

There was a breathy pause before Bob answered. "I'm not going to tell you how old she is. That way you won't make any judgments about her, judgments that would be wrong, at least as far as Johnny is concerned. If you don't know her calendar age, then she'll be as old as you make her."

"Look, Bob," I don't want to get Johnny a dog, have him fall in love with it—you know how he is with dogs—only to have his heart broken when she dies in a year or two. You don't want that either."

"Of course not," Bob said, sympathetically. "I wouldn't even suggest your taking her if I had a hint that she wouldn't be healthy—and active—for some years."

Then Bob added, "I'm not trying to butt into your life with your son. . . . Well, maybe I am," he admitted. "Anyway, you know how much I care about Johnny, so I might as well butt in a bit more. It's time for him to go off on his own and hunt with his own dog, not one of yours or mine. He should have a dog like this Lab for himself.

"By the way, her name is Belle."

*   *   *

"She's more than just a nice hunting dog," Belle's owner said to the two men and the boy. The dog sat calmly at his side as he spoke. "She's part of my family and my life. If there was any possible means for me to keep her, she'd be with me 'til she died. Unfortunately, there isn't any way for Belle to stay—maybe Bob told you why. If not, it doesn't matter. I'm just trying to find the best home I can for her, but it's hard to place a dog that's—"

Bob held up his hand and said quickly, "No age, remember?"

The man smiled and looked at John Sr. and his son. "Sorry, I forgot. Bob's right about not telling you her age. Belle's got some mileage on her body, but none on her heart. This dog has always had great heart." At her name, Belle turned her head and looked up at the man. He leaned over and rubbed her ears.

"I like the idea of Belle's going with you and your son. Bob's told me all that I need to know about both of you, and I trust his judgment. I especially like it because she'll be Johnny's dog.

I can't think of anything better for her."

The man petted Belle again, then snapped his fingers and said, "Okay." The Lab danced in front of him, waiting for something to happen.

"Johnny," he said, dragging the boy's attention off the cavorting dog, "why don't you take her into the field and fool around for a while. There might be a couple of pheasants hanging in that plum thicket over on the right. Just call her name, and she'll go with you."

The two of them left at a run—the dog in front, the boy behind. About fifty yards into the field, Johnny stopped and called Belle to him. He knelt and put his arms around her neck and appeared to speak into her ear. Belle nuzzled his neck, tentatively, then began to lick his face. The three men could hear the boy laughing. Again, Johnny hugged her tightly before standing. Belle moved to his side. He stroked her, then snapped his fingers and said, "Okay," just as he had seen the man do it.

Belle moved down the field with Johnny behind her. She caught a breeze and followed it, angling toward the plum thicket but never getting too far ahead of the boy. The dog tucked into the thicket, then came out of it at a run to push a hen pheasant into the air. At the flush, she dropped to a sit and watched the bird sail toward the next field.

"I'll bet this whole farm," Belle's owner said, grinning at the two men, "that he's telling her she's the best thing since sliced bread." The three of them had watched the episode unfold: the first hugs, the licks, Belle's flush and sit, then Johnny's walking to her for another series of pets and hugs.

"Well," Bob asked softly, "what do you think?"

"I think that Belle's found a home," John answered, without hesitation, still watching his son and the Labrador doing what boys and old dogs should do—have a good time and love each other. Nothing else, John decided at that moment —not even age—was important.

He looked at his friend, Bob, and nodded, then thrust out his hand to Belle's past owner. When the man took it, John Sr. said simply, "Thank you."

28

Welcome to Hard Times

He was a first-generation American, a springer spaniel of transplanted English parentage. From birth, he was destined to become a freewheeling good ol' boy—full of hell, with more than his share of screws loose, lacking the slightest suggestion of a stiff-lipped lord of the British manor.

Yes, he was born in the U.S.A. And together we had the days of seven seasons—not always great days, not always even acceptable days, but ever-interesting and occasionally monumental days.

Then he died here, much too soon, at not quite eight years old. At first, I thought that was why I ranked him so high on my personal short list of very good dogs: there hadn't been time to gain the wisdom of distance. Now, after enough years of separation, I know that wasn't the case.

He was wired motion—"supersonic," a friend tagged him—red hot and exceptionally athletic from the first. He ran with unmitigated flash, encumbered only by passion every step of his life, his liver-and-white body flowing like mercury behind a nose long with grouse and woodcock. This springer was indeed a damn Yankee, spontaneous and lacking the merest hint of moderation, born with a need to take life's corners on two wheels. He was a finished dog with a lilt in his gait and a let's-get-to-it attitude in his brain, a high-powered working stiff who showed up ready for every job and rarely failed to complete any of them. Until near the end. Then it was beyond him.

Toward the last days of what was to be his final bird season, the dog began to slow down. The change was almost imperceptible at first, no more than a mild tempering of his speed and his ability to bust brush. It wasn't a matter of willingness; his drive and push were there, but his body was showing signs of being elsewhere. When you live with a dog for seven years, you note such subtle shifts, especially in a springer who overrode pain and injury as a matter of course.

This was a dog who had hunted with a two-inch locust spine jammed to the hilt in the bones of his foot. He neither stopped to pull it out nor made a whimper over what must have been serious pain. When it became too much for him, he simply went up on three legs and continued to work until I whistled him to a stop and found the spine. This was a too-gritty springer that once hunted all morning, without a hitch in his step, on a pad gashed so badly that it later kept him off his feet for three weeks. I didn't find the cut until a normal, post-hunt exam, and from the damage it was clear that he had been running on it for hours. When such a single-minded dog tries to go but can't, however slight the signals, you look beyond the obvious.

I knew that something was wrong when he began walking in the final five to ten yards of his retrieves. After all, this was "supersonic," a spaniel who never walked; who would sit at a bird's flush and fall, leaning into it; and who, at his name, would rocket to the mark, pick it up in a pivoting cloud of dust, and be back in front of me before I could process what had just taken place. Walk on a retrieve?

Then, within a short period of time, he began to have a bit of trouble going up inclines. The first time his hindquarters caved in, on level ground, I had him in my veterinarian's office within a half-hour. His hips were perfect; besides, his troubles had developed too quickly and out of context for dysplasia. I assumed that his was a lower spinal problem, not entirely uncommon in fine-boned, superactive dogs.

Anal-gland cancer and its associated immediacy of mortality never occurred to me.

My vet, a friend, gave me an honest appraisal of the dog's condition and a straightforward look at my options—or, rather, my springer's options. None of them even approached being acceptable. This was a raging form of cancer that had leapfrogged from nothing to something to everything in a few months.

Discussions with veterinary oncologists pointed out just one thing and pointed it out quite clearly: Their ideas of successful treatment and mine were more than worlds apart. Surgery was their job; to me and my dog, this was personal. Full-scale treatment to gain perhaps an unpleasant month or two was something that had to be weighed against the unquestioned inevitable. Only the timing, not the end, was in doubt. My decision was both easy and difficult. This dog was born with élan and lived to run and hunt. I would not allow him to die as a pain-ridden shadow unable to rise from his bed.

The details of the last days are unimportant. Suffice it to say that they revolved around comfort and catering and a sense of the moment. I think, now, that I may have allowed those days to go on too long, but right and wrong, appropriate and inappropriate, can become hazy concepts that lack form and clear definition. Reality is a judgment of a point in time.

Woodcock were back in the spring coverts in numbers when that judgment came. Legality and penalties had no place in my thoughts when I entered a favored piece of cover and shot the first bird I found. My idea of the right thing to do had lifted me to a higher, or at least more immediate, moral level. Woodcock and I had been the two primary forces in this springer's life, and I intended him to have both close by his side as he left his seasons behind.

I drove back with the dog to that favorite covert—the one that he had hunted so well, so many times—and parked on an old logging road that led to its interior. We sat, or rather I sat while he curled next to me, on the truck's tailgate, where we had spent the time of seven years before and after hunts. The woodcock lay between his paws. He put his head on it and stared into the covert. Anything else was beyond his strength.

The sedative I gave him worked rapidly, and he was deeply asleep when we arrived at the vet's. My friend came out and did what was necessary as the spaniel slept in the truck with his head still on the woodcock and with my hand resting gently along the creamy curve of his neck.

Welcome to hard times.

The stiff wind rolling off the river blew this springer spaniel's ashes, blended inseparably with those of the last woodcock of his short life, through the alders and into the abutting pines. The gray-white cloud did not linger in the breeze, though it hung for a moment against the dark of the conifers. Then it took off and was gone.

I think that my hard-going springer would have appreciated the quickness of his ashes' departure. During his seasons as a freewheeling gun dog, he hadn't been one to linger when it was time to go.

29
The Flight

The early air had an edge to it—not so sharp that it razored through clothing, but keen enough to nick ears and cheeks. Here and there, chilled beads of the previous night's rain dripped from the trees and fell earthward through a full palette of October color. A breeze sighed up the maple-lined lane, gently stirring the dying ferns clustered along deep-puddled ruts and swaying more raindrops off the needles of scattered pines.

By midmorning, the light wind, bolstered by a building sun, would dry all but the most shaded pockets of cover. But for a time, the canopy and its understory were wet enough to dampen hat, boots, and legs; soak the fur of a dog; and hold bird scent for that dog to work.

Altogether, the man thought with a hint of a satisfied smile playing across his face, it was a fine morning to be poking into the quiet heart of a woodcock covert. Especially one that he and his setter knew so well. There would be no preliminary examination, no prodding, no feeling for the covert's pulse before getting a grip on how to hunt it. If woodcock had come on the overnight front, the dog would find them.

The man paused and stood motionless in the old lane's track. He smiled again, this time inside, more for himself than anything else. He turned slowly, pivoting first down the lane toward the river, then looking back beneath the canopied archway of it. He stared into the trees to the sides, at the tumbledown stone wall that peeked through them, gleaming a dappled gray touched with moss green in the slanting rays of sun.

He squinted to find the rock foundation of the house that had once stood on the far side of the wall and to see the age-bent apple trees that backed up to it. The leaves were still too thick, but he knew where it was, all of it, and how it looked on clean and weightless mornings like this. And that is what made him smile. This section of land was laid out like an artist's too-perfect rendering of how a woodcock covert should look. It seemed ready-made, not by Nature but by a hunter's idealized concept of Nature. Each time the man hunted here, he felt as though he had stepped out of life and onto a painter's canvas. All he needed to complete the image were the weavings of his dog and the flush of woodcock.

His season had been slow to that point. It had been too warm and dry, with October following the lead of a September weather pattern of high temperatures and no moisture. Neither condition tended to move woodcock through his piece of the north country. The man and his dog had hunted hard for few woodcock, picking up occasional birds tucked along creeks and seeps, and snugged tight under pines—anywhere there was the merest spit of dampness.

It was then, in the first days of that unseasonable October, that the man realized his setter was old. The weather bothered the dog; it weakened and exhausted him and forced him into the creeks for frequent drinks and coolings. But it was more than just the heat. The white dog, his dark head split by the wide blaze that gave him his name, was twelve years old and seemed to have fallen into old age suddenly, almost overnight, though the man knew that it had not happened that way. This setter had never been a "greased-lightening" sort of dog but, rather, was paced and sensible when he ran the cover. Now, he was even more prudent and calculating in his movements and bird work.

The man whistled softly from the roadway, so low that a human fifty feet into the woods couldn't have heard it. The old setter pushed out of the brush, ambled purposefully up the ruts to the man's left leg where he stood, waiting. The dog's only motions were tiltings of his head to catch the ground breeze and tremors that rippled along the muscles of his back and down his stringy hindquarters.

"At least your hearing is still good," the man said as he bent to scratch the leathery ears. He moved his fingers down the wet fur of the blaze between the dog's eyes to the heavy muzzle, where rich black was salted with white. "Relax a minute," he whispered, kneeling by the dog's side. "We've got time. If birds are here, they'll wait for us."

The sun had stretched to the treetops when the man snapped his fingers to the left and cast the setter toward the stone wall and the old farmstead. He watched the white dog climb a low spot in the wall—not clear it with a leap as he would have a few seasons past—and move at a slow, head-high lope through a young aspen stand that had invaded the edges of the caved-in foundation. The dog circled the echoing depths of a defunct well and gave a wide berth to a trash pit—a junk collector's El Dorado of discarded farm and home debris, blue bottles, and rust-crumbling cans. Then the setter shifted upwind of a dense cluster of whippy, thumb-sized birch trees.

The man watched him slow down, creep two discreet steps forward, then freeze. His tail lifted straight, like a thinly feathered finger pointing skyward. The dog's head was thrust out, aimed at the birches, in an exact plane with his body. The man walked rapidly around him into the birch thicket, where the spindly limbs clutched at his jacket and whipped against his shooting glasses. He was pulling his boot from a root tangle when a woodcock twittered up, leveled above the trees, and disappeared. A second bird jumped, then two more, and—finally—a fifth. This one tumbled to earth through a flurry of feathers. Other than head shifts that let him mark the birds' flush lines, the setter did not budge until his name was called for the retrieve.

"We've got some birds in here, old fella," the man said to the dog after taking the woodcock and admiring it for a moment, "Looks like a flight dropped in last night." He let the setter nose the bird, then eased it into his game bag. "Let's find a couple more before the wind dries everything up."

In less than an hour, without hunting more than a hundred yards from the foundation, they moved twenty-eight more woodcock. Although some of the flushes were wild and others were multiples off the same find, the old white setter righteously pinned eleven of those birds. But it was in the uncluttered apple orchard with its gnarled trees from another time that the dog shined and added the essential brush strokes of his work to the unfinished canvas the man saw in his mind's eye.

The setter had drifted gently over the dampish earth like a weaving trail of smoke following a hint of breeze—pausing here, stopping there, whisping his unobtrusive way through the orchard's nooks and crannies. He was workmanlike but not overly methodical; deliberate, but not pottering; cautious but not tentative. He was unrattled by so many birds and so much scent. Watching him, the man realized that on this day, a younger, more high-spirited and exuberant dog would have been out of context, perhaps even an intrusion in this perfect cover.

Moving about the orchard, following a dog that he had trained and hunted for twelve years, the man realized something else. This white setter with the wide blaze was without doubt the best bird dog he had ever owned—and had been the best for years, long before age slowed him. He understood, as well, that he had taken this fine dog for granted, that he had allowed himself to see the setter's day-in, day-out, season-after-season performances as commonplace, as the expected rather than the singular.

The man shot a limit of woodcock that morning out of choice, something he had not done for at least five years. He shot them because he had to, for his setter. Meaningless as he knew the gesture was, he saw it as his sole way of acknowledging to the dog what had gone unacknowledged for so many years. He shot them, too, for his memory, to keep a poignant morning alive and vivid in his mind, stored against a time not that far ahead when the dog would no longer add his grace to the covert.

The two of them finished their morning back at the stone wall. The man sat on a mossy rock watching fluffs of cloud drift across what was, by now, a soft-pastel sky. The setter lay on ferns with his grizzled head draped on a leather boot. The air had warmed and the earth had dried, as the man knew they would. But that didn't matter. The morning had stayed chilled and wet just long enough.

Epilogue

Perfect
Mornings

It seems fitting that I end *Gun Dog Chronicles* in the same month and physical space in which I began it. Indeed, the similarity of time and place brings a degree of symmetry to an otherwise relatively unsymmetrical life. It allows me to come full circle and simplifies the job of wrapping up the frayed ends of thoughts and musings that have occupied me for the better part of a year. Stay with me for a moment, if you will.

It is a perfect autumn morning, and I am sitting in the "Bear's Den," a small, squarish building on my home property. With walls, floor, and fireplace of Maine granite, it is nestled at the edge of a mature oak stand, overlooking a small pond. Two dozen Canada geese graze around the water's edge.

This building, the den, is well over a half-century old and was once used as a working getaway by the original "Bear," an internationally known writer of considerably greater stature than I'll ever attain. But I am not in the Bear's Den to gain inspiration from another. I am here for visual comfort and a peace-of-mind setting conducive to recapitulation.

Above me, on a thick ceiling beam, rests a saddle, a personal relic of another time. Its leather is shiny from use and still holds the sweetish smell of oil and horse sweat. Hand-braided reins, a Mexican hackamore, and a horsehair rope hang from its horn. Worn stirrups fall slightly below hat level and crack my distracted skull as I pace the uneven floor stones. Old duck calls and dog whistles dangle at the ends of lanyards hanging in a cluster from a heavy wall support. Above the rough fireplace hangs a print featuring two English setters down hard on a quail covey. The original oil was painted by my artist-friend Ross Young, and this signed gift of his work has found a fine home on the den's granite. A model 1897 Winchester, a "cornshucker" pump gun, tops the print.

Two springer spaniels are with me in the Bear's Den. They are the most prominent parts of the setting but are far more than ornamental. I can do without the other stuff but not without the motivating presence of the dogs. One of them is young, just three years old, and remains aggravatingly immature. He pads from corner to corner, investigating floor and wall crevices that he has already nosed ad nauseum.

My other spaniel is thirteen and has long since gained the wisdom to follow his body's dictates and relax when he has the chance. He lies stretched and twitching in sleep on a rug directly in front of the door—to prevent my departing alone should his aging eyes and ears fail him. Age has taught him the importance of position, and he uses the strategy well, just as he did in his final seasons afield.

Perhaps now you understand why I have returned to the splendid solitude of the Bear's Den to complete what I started here months ago. I fill my coffee mug from a stained pot and slouch down in a chair, my head leaned against its back. The young springer moves to me, oddly placid for once, and lays his muzzle on my knee. Perhaps it is his expression that captures my mind or the tilt of his eyes as he stares up at me or the fingering beam of early sun that strokes his liver-and-white head. Maybe it is all of those things, along with subtleties that beggar definition, that pull me backward with images of another springer on another morning not that long past, a morning that was a gift whose minutes and hours flowed together into an extraordinary whole.

*   *   *

I don't know what perfection means, at least in terms of real events, but when I think that I might be seeing it, I have enough sense to grab the moments and lock them firmly in memory. Definition and detail can be sorted out later, during another season, a less-full season that offers the wider perspective of time.

Clouds layered away on the horizon, grimy stacks of them piled high by winds at the far edge of sight. Overhead, the sky was a flawless blue. An autumnal front had barged through in the night, lashed tight to the backside of a hard rain, and dragged a swath of stunningly clear air behind it. It was cold for early October, but the day was warming under the weight of a sun that danced on the melt of the first hard frost.

My springer was drenched with frost water from his flaring brown nose to his white, windmilling tail, which flung droplets in his wake. He was making game. Woodcock, goosed south by the front, were in the coverts in numbers but were scattered, which allowed the dog to hunt singles rather than collections of scent. His pattern took him in and out of my sight in the sprawl of leafy thickness; at times only the tinkling bell told me his location and speed. He was a seven-year-old dog, a well-seasoned veteran with hundreds of flushes under his collar, but on that chill, wet, scent-rich morning he became part of the land. He owned the covert and every woodcock in it.

From choice, I shot just one nicely worked bird before we struck an old farm track and eased down to a sliver of creek bracketed by an alder run where southering woodcock often dropped in to rest.

To me, there is a different level of quality between a single act—like a classic point or flush or retrieve—and an impeccable day, a day without seams, a day so symmetrical and complete that it can't be faulted.

The first bird we moved in the deep alders was created for an on-fire dog. It was a runner that weaved an unusually long and devious trail—scooting straight, then darting to the sides, backtracking, short-flushing for a few yards, then hotfooting again. When the cover opened up, I saw pieces of the drama, like segments of choreography: the running woodcock, the nose-down springer, his loss of scent, the dog's quick circling to ferret out the trail, his stops to the whistle when I fell behind in the tangles. Then there was the finale of a high-angling flush and the dog stretching and twisting in the air, grabbing for feathers.

But the bird swapped ends in mid-jump and lined back at me no more than a yard overhead before towering out of the trees and sideslipping toward a far aspen slope that hemmed the alder run. My full-pivoting, off-balance shot turned out to be the longest I had ever made on a woodcock, a bit over forty yards. It translated into a longer, blind retrieve for the steady springer, now hupped behind me and buried in screening cover.

I don't question the theoretical how of that trailing race; the driving, airborne flush; the extraordinary retrieve—it remains in my mind as a unique ballet of two. But I still wonder at the actual why of it. Maybe because it involved a woodcock, usually not the most dramatic bird for a hard-going dog. Possibly, it was destined to be part of a quintessential morning, a lone episode that was extraordinary by itself, but superb when joined with others of its kind into a perfect total.

Often, perhaps too often, I think back on certain fine days seeking defects overlooked in my first rush to judgment. As yet, I have found none—not even a hairline crack—that might fracture the wholeness of that day.

My springer had flowed through the coverts for hours, hunting smoothly without a hitch, without a whistle other than stop signals, without a voice command other than my calling his name for a retrieve, without the touch of my hand other than caressing strokes for a fine job. He had worked fast and sharp, closing his pattern in heavy brambles and alders, pushing it out in open orchards. Every flush was hard and steady, each retrieve was straight and clean. And the morning finished as it began, as a time to be held tightly.

Autumn cloaked the forenoon earth. The air had warmed to a softness and—in concert with a lilting ground breeze—had burned the frost from all but shaded nooks. The sun-soaked foliage was so keen it hurt my eyes. Its colors were so pure I could almost taste them: the sharp spice of crimsons, the subtle herb of yellows, the light syrup of magentas. Woodsmoke fingered-in from somewhere and blended with a hint of tidepool from the miles-off seacoast.

Perfection? No, I can't define it. Not even for myself, on my own terms. But if I didn't see it on this morning revisited, then at the least I have an eloquent standard by which to judge the beauty and immensity of other mornings. By any measure, it was a gift.

More fine sporting titles from Silver Quill Press

Feisty Little Pointing Dog
Edited by David Webb

Equally at home pointing woodcock on the soft ground of New England alder thickets and scenting chukar partridge on the swirling winds of western mountains, the Brittany is first and foremost, a gun dog. The breed's skill and, occasionally, antics afield are wonderfully told in the twenty-six stories that comprise this tribute. Includes black-and-white line drawings by Chris Smith. Hardcover.

Training Retrievers and Spaniels to Hunt 'em Up!
by Joe Arnette and George Hickox

Hunt 'em Up! is written for American bird hunters, from the American perspective. Here, you'll find invaluable insight into the canine mind and how your pup learns, followed by a clear, logical, step-by-step training program that has succeeded time and time again in producing superb gun dogs. You will discover that you can end up with a fine hunting dog by training it yourself. Hardcover.

Handy to Home
A Lifetime in the Maine Outdoors
by Tom Hennessey

For decades, writer and artist Tom Hennessey has fished, hunted, camped, canoed, and snowshoed in the woods of his native Maine. In *Handy to Home*, we have assembled the very best of Tom's work—his essays, his black-and-white illustrations, and, for the first time ever in book form, twelve of his stunning watercolors, all of them produced specifically for this book. Hardcover.

-more-

Traveler's Tales
The Wanderings and of a Bird Hunter and Sometime Fly Fisherman
by Michael McIntosh

McIntosh's name has become a virtual household word among sportsmen through his columns in sporting magazines. Deserving a place in the library of every sportsman, *Traveler's Tales* is, nonetheless, much more than a fishing and hunting book. In his trademark relaxed, readable style, McIntosh explores not only the fascinating places he has gone afield with rod or gun, but also the people he has gone with. Hardcover.

The Gun Review Book
by Michael McIntosh

In The Gun-Review Book, McIntosh discusses "What's New" in the world of both custom-made and production guns, then proceeds to "What's Old but Still Available," and rounds out the text with "Guns for the Game: Sporting Clays." Paperback.

Bush Pilot Angler
A Memoir
by Lee Wulff

Based on an unpublished manuscript that was uncovered only recently by his widow, this extraordinary memoir tells the story of the years in which Lee pioneered the fabulous salmon and brook trout fisheries on the remote coast of Newfoundland. He flew a Piper J3 Cub on floats and ferried "sports" into isolated lakes and rivers where the fishing exceeded their wildest dreams. Bush Pilot Angler is a marvelous story of courage, love, flying, and fishing. Hardcover

Available in bookstores, or by calling Silver Quill Press at:
1-800-685-7962

Find our catalog on the world wide web at:
www.downeastbooks.com